TREND FOLLOWING STOCKS

How to Trade Stocks Profitably in any Market

Jesse P. Webb

TRENDS UNIVERSITY

Published by Market Harbinger Institute LLC – Publishing division
www.mhillc.org

Authored by Jesse Webb
Cover design by Dan DeCort
decortinteractive.com
Editing by Cynthia Regenhold

www.TrendFollowingStocks.com
www.MarketTrendSignal.com
www.TrendsUniversity.com

Printed in the United States of America

First Printing: April 2010

ISBN-13   978-0-9845212-0-3
ISBN-10   0-9845212-0-8

Contents

Market Trend Signal™
Market Timing - Trend Following - Stock Ratings

Contents

Market Trend Signal™
Market Timing - Trend Following - Stock Ratings

Contents

Overview

Trend following is a trading concept that challenges your thinking and increases trading intelligence. The name of this game is strength and trend. The practice of trend following is buying stocks that are already moving up in price. Trend following challenges the "buy and hold" status quo mechanics because it provides a better way to systematically detect market and stock direction. Couple this view with the MTS™ system and you have the tools to not only gain a visual perspective of market direction, but also how particular stocks are currently performing. And it doesn't stop there.

Why and how is trend following your edge? Both questions can be answered with the dual integrity of MTS™ detection and trend following methodology. Trend following is based on a system of risk control and money management and the MTS™ system is a trading application that searches for qualified, high-ranking stocks that reports (on demand) specific trade entry and exit signals. Within the pages of this book, they're groomed to seamlessly work together. While MTS™ can stand alone (being built on the concept of "unlimited" upside stock potential), the concept of trend following combined with MTS™ gives you the insight you need to confidently trade stocks, ETFs, and Forex, profitably.

This book describes the "hand-in-hand" combination of trend following with the MTS™ system. You can expect to delve into the MTS™ system to understand and use formulas and strategies, identify and analyze trend patterns, perform back testing, find trade expectancy, and evaluate probabilities. You'll be introduced to MTS™ *MuscleStocks* which are a group of predefined Buy rated stocks—stocks that are the cream of the crop.

We're confident that trend following using the MTS™ system will put you ahead of the crowd, and ahead of the curve. Welcome to the first day of your next successful trade.

TRENDS UNIVERSITY

Chapter 1
Trend Following Stocks

Contents

It is commonly believed that the definition of insanity is doing the same thing over and over and expecting different results. Are you consistently losing money in the market? Are you able to determine your risk on every trade? Do you constantly find yourself on the wrong side of every trade? Do you really "know" what you are doing, or are you really just throwing darts? Do you analyze the bad trades you made to the point of madness, yet you turn around and make the exact same mistake all over again? Are you able to sleep at night? Do you hope the bleeding of a lost trade will stop soon? Do you do anything about it? Do you buy more of your losers and sell your winners too quickly? Do you "think" that buying a stock that has already had a major move higher is "wrong" or not effective?

If you ask yourself these questions and can answer 'yes' to all or most of them, then you are definitely in the right place. If you have the desire to consistently be on the working side of every trade, if you will follow a strict set of rules, and if you throw everything you have ever learned (that hasn't worked for you) out the window, this method and system will work for you.

Rethinking the Basics

The first thing I want you to do is throw out all your expectations. Clear your head of the current size of your trading or bank account. Clear your head of the size you want that account to be one year or 10 years from now. Expectations of what you want to happen will be your first failure. You may have already experienced this to some degree in your investing and trading. You may have felt the pressure of success or the pressure of failure. Free your mind from this very minute of what you want to happen or what you think "should" happen. Sounds kind of "Zen-like," right? Well it is. The mental aspect of trading can be the single most important factor of success or failure.

Many traders confuse profitable trading with the need to be right. The need to be right is so strong for many people; they confuse it with a system of analysis. You may think to yourself, 'this stock is going to go up!' This idea has nothing to do with what is currently happening. Traders that think the stock should go up just because they bought it are the same people that think they are going to eventually hit the jackpot. Trading and making money have nothing to do with education level, ability to analyze, or the perceived "skill" of picking the top or bottom. No matter how many income statements you read or growth projections you massage, your chances of having a successful trade based on knowing that information still may not be any better than 50/50.

Trend Following is Your Edge

Trend following is a reactive trading method. It does not anticipate a move before it happens. It does not forecast or predict future price levels or price movements. It involves a risk management system that uses the current market-driven price direction. Trend trading requires that you have strict discipline to follow precise rules. Trend followers use an initial risk rule that determines the size of their position at the time of entry. This means you know exactly how many shares of stock to buy or sell based on how much money you have. Changes in price may lead to an increase or decrease of your initial trade. Adverse price movements may lead to an exit for your entire trade. This can take place in a week or in a year, depending on the strength of the trend. Historically, a trend follower's average profit per trade is significantly higher than the average loss per trade. You will see how this is also the case using MTS™.

Trend following is not a crystal ball. It is not a fad or magical approach, either. Beyond the mere rules, the human element is critical to the system. It takes intense discipline and emotional will to stick with trend trading through the inevitable market ups and downs. Trend following traders expect ups and downs and plan for them in advance.

Trend following is a methodology of trading. There are many different strategies to use within this methodology. Most strategies are simple to employ yet very difficult for some to stick with. The concept is simple: stay in a trend as long as it is there.

Trend following is a systematic approach to trading stocks. It is a systematic method as opposed to a discretionary approach. System trading is technical by nature, meaning that trade decisions are either based on a *system* of price or based on indicators of price alone. There are almost as many systems as there are traders. Some systems work and others don't. Some are easy to use while some are very difficult. Systematic trading takes discipline, trust and patience. System traders understand two things very well. They will have drawdown (periods of losses), and they also know that trusting their system will offer gains in the future. You see, what happens to most traders is they want to find the crystal ball...the holy grail of trading and making money. Once they believe they have found this "holy grail," it inevitably changes and the trader must move on in search of the next crystal ball. The cycle ends when the trader is out of money.

Discretionary approaches imply that *you* are the edge. You somehow have a sixth sense about trades and have a lighting fast method to squash the market. You know exactly what you're looking for and you decide when the stock is about to catapult to monstrous gains. You have cat-like reflexes as your eyes bulge bloodshot at three monitors and your caffeinated, twitching, trigger finger gets super punchy at any tick on your level-two day-trading account! "You" are the guru. How's that been working for you? How many times has your guru senses changed during a losing streak? How many times have you swung for the fences because you believed that *this* is the one? Well, there is a better, less stressful way to gain your edge.

Price is Paramount

Price contains all information. Information that is known and anticipated is already priced into the stock. There are billions of dollars invested every day in stocks by large institutional investors. These institutions do their homework. They kick the tires, they poke and prod. They crunch numbers then crunch them again, then have computers crunch them yet again, all in hopes of finding an edge—the edge that will explain to them why the investment they are about to make is undervalued or a good investment. They will not buy unless there is some determination as to current valuation. Once there is a consensus that there is an opportunity to buy, they will buy—and buy heavily. Large institutions don't buy in one shot like the rest of us. They may spend days or weeks accumulating a position. When this happens, trends are created. Whether they're correct in their analysis is completely irrelevant to us.

Valuation is a fleeting term. Everyone has their own explanation of what valuation is and why it's important to making money. There's a common misconception that in order to get a good stock, it needs to have a low price/earnings (PE) ratio. Interpretation opens up a hundred other so-called "fundamental" questions that are very subjective. Then there is the argument that growth stocks "deserve" a higher PE because their earnings are growing much more quickly than a "value" stock, and so on. What you will learn in this book is that the bottom line is making money. I want you to find stocks and trades that will make you money and a lot of it. I don't care what the PE is or what the profit margins are, or what the growth projections are, or what hot shot analyst has the stock rated. If it's a strong stock and it's trending higher, I want in.

The point is: institutions move markets. You and I don't need to know one thing about any company. You don't even need to know the name of the company. All you need is a system that lets you know if there is an opportunity. Trend following is piggy-backing. We are, in the most simplistic terms, piggy-backing on power hitters' trading! It's a beautiful thing.

One of the first rules of trend following is that price is paramount. Price rules. Price tells all. If a stock is at 300 and goes to 270, 250, and then 230, the stock is trending downward. Despite what the financial news shows say or what analysts might predict, if the trend is down, you stay with the trend. You need only be concerned with what the

4

stock is doing, not what the stock *might* do. The price tells you what the stock is doing. Think about some of the stocks that were considered strong and stable a few short years ago. Stocks like GM, Bear Stearns, Lehman Brothers, WaMu, and Fannie Mae were almost considered national icons. The down trends in their stock told you all you needed to know. Why did you feel inclined to continue to hold them into the ground? Did you fall for the mainstream myth that stocks will always bounce back?

The single most valuable piece of information systematic trading gives is structure. System trading is based on following rules and doing it the same way consistently. If you're a rule breaker or if you feel like rules don't apply to you, then you will struggle.

Trend Following is Systematic

Trend traders don't expect to be right on every trade. In fact, trend followers are the best losers you will meet. There is no marriage to a trade and no ego about being right or wrong. There are simply rules to follow. Some trades result in gains and some result in losses, but trend traders will take losses quickly before having it turn into a major loss. Learning to take a loss is one thing, but learning *when* and *how* to take one is much more valuable. The most critical factor of trend following is not the timing of the trade or the indicator, nor is it the method or system. Rather, the most critical factor is determining how much to trade over the course of the trend.

Trend following is based on a system of controlling risk and managing money. The risk control system is easy to learn. During periods of higher market volatility, your trading size is reduced. During losing periods, your positions are reduced and your trade size is cut back. The main objective is to preserve your capital until more favorable price trends reappear. Cutting losses quickly is the only way to stay in the game.

Trend followers do not wait to see their losses recover. They exit systematically with no emotion attached to the trade. If the stock bottoms then trends back up, the new price trend creates a new Buy signal, which they employ to make a new trade.

Trend following is systematic. Price and trend are critical at all times. Trend following is not based on an analysis of fundamental supply and demand factors. Trend following

does *not* involve magical patterns, points and figures, market profiles, triangles, or day trading mechanics. Charts and signals are easy to read and understand. If you have to spend more than a half an hour a day on your trades, you're spending too much time. We do not day trade, we actually make money.

Trading to Win with the MTS™ System

People generally lose money in the market for one reason only. They're always on the wrong side of the trend. This happens because they accept as "gospel" age old investment advice such as "buy and hold." Millions of investors, possibly you included, have fallen prey to this antiquated, broken system which has caused untold heartache and the loss of millions of hard-earned dollars.

Instead of having clearly defined entry and exit strategies for protecting your money, you may find that you're listening to proponents of buy and hold advice. You may make investment decisions under the guise of their "sound investment principles." Their suggestions are based on ideas such as, "It's time in the market—not timing the market," or, "Hang in there...we're near a bottom," and even, "No one can time the market successfully, so why try?" Have you heard any of those lines before? We all used to believe the earth was flat, too. Buy and hold investing is simply an excuse for laziness and incompetence.

You've heard the story of why you should buy a handful of great American companies, lock them away in a safety deposit box and wait thirty years before looking at them again. I know some of you have had that experience. Maybe it was GM or Ford, IBM, GE, Disney, or AT&T. Many of these companies have made many millionaires in this country, it is true, but it all depends on where these investors bought in. Most people buy at the wrong time and do not have any rhyme or reason for buying or selling.

Buying and Selling the Trend

I have an example of what can happen to an investor who trades versus using buy and hold investing.

The chart in Figure 1.1 shows a buy and hold example for (TEN) Tenneco, Inc., a company in the motor vehicle parts and accessories industry. We can see that the stock experienced a rapid rise followed by a horrific plunge. The chart shows activity from 2000 to early 2009. Let's say you took a ten thousand dollar position in this stock beginning on May 9, 2000 at the purchase price of $8.38. We can see that the stock value sank to $0.65 a year and a half later. Over the next six years, it rocketed to nearly $40.00. It suffered along with the auto industry and crashed to a low of $0.42 on March 2, 2009. Then, true to form, it was resurrected again and blasted to nearly eighteen dollars, settling at $15.19 on November 11, 2009—just seven short months off the $0.42 lows!

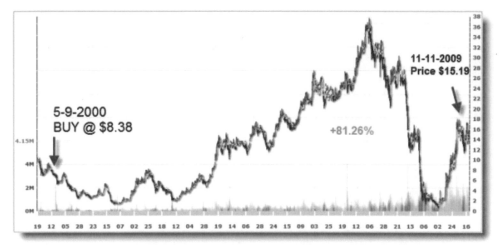

Figure 1.1. Tenneco Inc (TEN) showing buy and hold example.

What a ride! Would you have held the whole time? Would you have felt the pain at $0.42 and bailed out? How about bailing the first time at $0.65 and missing the whole ride? Had you stuck it out, you would have turned ten thousand dollars into $18,126—a gain of 81.26%. If you did, then congratulations! You're an astute buy and hold investor; you've made a nice profit on your funds. But, oh, what you missed if you decided to bail, when all you needed was just a little bit of savvy.

Now, take the exact same stock, the exact same conditions, circumstances, and beginning investment amount, and add one new dynamic: you buy and sell along the way. What a novel idea. Let's see how you did.

Using the MTS™ trading signals and only buying on the Buy signals and exiting on the Sell signals, you would have grown your ten thousand dollar investment to $807,661 profit in nine years, providing a 111.96% annual trade expectancy. In Figure 1.2, we can see that thirty trades were generated—an average of just three trades per year! The average gain per trade is 94.34% and the average loss per trade was 9.59% which is a reward to risk ratio of 9.84:1. That, very simply, is what trading versus "buy and hold" will do for you.

Trade Stats for	**TEN**		Current Signal	Buy
Number of Trades		30	Trade expectancy	$3,544.97
Total Profit amount		$927,211.03	Trade expectancy%	35.45%
Total Loss amount		$119,549.62	Annual Trade expectancy	$11,196.25
Net Profit/Loss		$807,661.41	Annual Trade expectancy%	111.96%
Avg Profit on Winners		$71,323.93	Largest profit	$463,532.16
Avg Loss on Losers		$7,032.33	Largest loss	$17,421.93
Total Net % gain or loss		8076.61%	Avg days in trade	62
Aver % gain on Winners		94.34%	Avg days between trades	53
Aver % loss on Losers		9.59%		
Reward to Risk Ratio		9.84		
Number of Trades Per year		3.2		
Number of Winners		13		
Number of Losers		17		
Winning Percentage		43.33		

Start date	05/09/2000		End date	11/11/2009	

Figure 1.2. Tenneco Inc (TEN) showing long only example.

Now, that was just the "long only" example, meaning you *only* bought on the Buy signals and you sold those shares on the Sell signals. If you used a long/short strategy (buying on the Buy signals then selling on the Sell signals) and *also* shorted on the same Sell signal, then the performance results you would have experienced would have been astounding. With fifty-nine total trades, 6 per year—that's one trade every other month, folks—the average gain per trade is 60.39% and the average loss per trade was

10.14%...a reward to risk ratio of 5.96:1 (*see* Figure 1.3). The total return in nine years is 22,390%, turning ten thousand dollars into $2,239,009 of net profit!

Trade Stats for	**TEN**	Current Signal	Buy
Number of Trades	59	**Trade expectancy**	$2,094.40
Total Profit amount	$2,679,221.69	**Trade expectancy%**	20.94%
Total Loss amount	$440,212.12	**Annual Trade expectancy**	$13,009.19
Net Profit/Loss	$2,239,009.57	**Annual Trade expectancy%**	130.09%
Avg Profit on Winners	$103,046.99	**Largest profit**	$1,404,073.49
Avg Loss on Losers	$13,339.76	**Largest loss**	$148,371.40
Total Net % gain or loss	22390.10%	**Avg days in trade**	
Aver % gain on Winners	60.39%	**Avg days between trades**	
Aver % loss on Losers	10.14%		
Reward to Risk Ratio	5.96		
Number of Trades Per year	6.2		
Number of Winners	26		
Number of Losers	33		
Winning Percentage	44.07		

Start date	05/09/2000		**End date**	11/11/2009	

Figure 1.3. Tenneco Inc (TEN) showing long and short example.

If you think this example is a bit extreme and doesn't really represent reality, let me show you an example of one of the worst stocks you could have owned in the past ten years and how it has performed using MTS™ (*see* Figures 1.4 and 1.5).

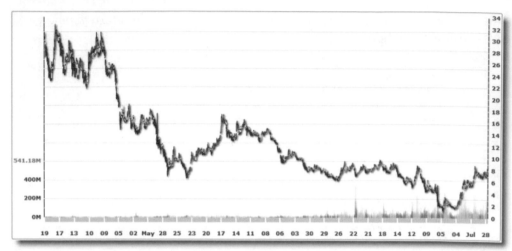

Figure 1.4. Ford Motor (F) chart showing long and short example.

Trade Stats for	F	Current Signal	Buy
Number of Trades	81	Trade expectancy	$352.89
Total Profit amount	$103,317.15	Trade expectancy%	3.52%
Total Loss amount	$64,596.05	Annual Trade expectancy	$2,788.55
Total Profit or Total Loss	$38,721.09	Annual Trade expectancy%	27.89%
Avg Profit on Winners	$2,951.92	Largest profit	$22,645.98
Avg Loss on Losers	$1,404.26	Largest loss	$5,124.78
Total Net % gain or loss	387.21%		
Aver % gain on Winners	17.18%		
Aver % loss on Losers	6.85%		
Reward to Risk Ratio	2.51		
Number of Trades Per year	7.9		
Number of Winners	35		
Number of Losers	46		
Winning Percentage	43.21		

Back Test | Equity Curve | StockSymbol f

Please select buy/sell criteria

☑ Long

Buy — Sell —

☑ Short

Sell — Buy —

Investment dollars: 10000

Additions on Signals

☑ Compound original invesment

☐ Use fixed amount on new signal

Query

Start date 01/01/2000 End date 03/23/2010

Figure 1.5. Ford Motor (F) chart showing long and short trades over the past 10 years. The annual trade expectancy is over 27% per year.

Using MTS™ to guide your trading of Ford for the past ten years, and using a long/short trading method, you could have made nearly 400% on a stock that has been in a ten year down trend.

TRENDS UNIVERSITY

The point here is with almost as much effort as it takes to log into an account as a buy and hold investor, you can buy and sell along the way and not just increase your returns, but also realize real staggering wealth. This is where it starts to get exciting.

Notes and Comments

Notes and Comments

TRENDS
UNIVERSITY

Notes and Comments

Chapter 2
What is Market Trend Signal™?

Contents

Market Trend Signal™ (MTS™) is a trading system used to implement the concepts of trend following. MTS™ is a systematic trading application that searches for qualified, high-ranking stocks, gives traders specific trade entry and exit signals, and provides traders with insight and strategy to confidently trade stocks, ETFs and Forex profitably. It has been proven that traders gain a much higher probability of having successful, profitable trades when trading in the same direction of the market, and when using a fixed set of rules. This chapter will define what Market Trend Signal™ considers the "market," explain how market direction is determined, and introduce the MTS™ Stock Screener and other analysis tools designed to enhance trading decisions.

The Market Trend Signal™ system works from a top-down approach. The order of the system is as follows:

- Market direction,
- StrengthRank™ to find leadership,
- Stock direction,

- Money management,
- Trade decision, and
- Trade management.

Your goal is to make money. It is not necessary to be right every time or to be the smartest or the quickest. I hope this isn't a rude awakening, but there will always be someone faster, smarter and quicker than you. You'll never be the first one in a trade at the bottom and you'll never be the first out at the top. If you feel this intense desire to be right and prove your brilliance to the market, the market will quickly bring you to your knees in humble submission.

Investors who buy stocks as they are falling in price and sell stocks when they are going up in price are often swimming against the current. While swimming against the current is possible, it's not very efficient or productive. Buying stocks on the way down is a loser's game and it's the fastest possible way to separate yourself from your cash. Dollar cost averaging (buying as prices drop, thus lowering your average cost) may work in some cases when buying mutual funds, but when trading stocks it is a very risky strategy to employ. As we move through the next several chapters, you'll clearly see why.

The name of this trading game is strength and trend. You want to buy stocks that are already moving higher. You want to only buy stocks that are already "working" i.e., already moving in the direction you want them to go. As a new trend follower, this may seem hard at first, but given the right market environment, you'll discover that it is really like printing money.

Many trend following systems are designed to work trading futures and Forex markets. While these objectives are integrated into the MTS™ framework, the trader's perspective is focused primarily on trend following stocks.

The power of the MTS™ system is built on the concept of "unlimited" upside stock potential. Theoretically, a stock can go up forever. In reality, we know that is not the case. Still, potential exists where strong trending stocks can increase thousands of percent in a single trend that may last only a year to 18 months. Hands down, the right kind of non-leveraged stock based on pure percentage, when traded like its own market, can outperform any futures or Forex market when it is in an up-trending trajectory. You will see many of these examples throughout the book.

Time Frame Signals

Before I lay out the steps to the system, let's get familiar with MTS™ signals. Market Trend Signal™ offers three distinct trending time frames. The first is the long term trend or simply what we call the "LT trend." This is a measure of trend for approximately 180 trading days or six months and is a very slow-moving trend.

The second time frame is the rating. MTS™ gives BUY, SELL and HOLD ratings for stocks. The term "Buy" simply means the stock is trending higher and could be purchased. The term "Hold" means don't buy if you don't own and don't sell if you do own. "Sell" means chuck it, bail, toss it…you get the picture.

The best time to actually make a trade is when the rating is shifting from Sell to Buy or Hold to Buy. This gives you the best position to catch an early trend. When the system signals SELL, it's time to get out of the stock. Your first loss is your best loss. There is no point on waiting to see if it will find support and then move higher. When you're waiting, you are hoping it will go higher. Hope is *not* a tool used for effective and profitable trading.

The last time frame is the shortest duration which is used in a short term trend or "ST trend." The time frame focuses on a 7-15 day trend and gives either an UP or DN signal.

The Market Trend Signal™ Trading System

Step One: Market Direction Dictates the Trade

The market is made up of individual stocks. It should make sense if the market is falling, a large group of stocks is also falling, and it's actually what is making the market fall. It should also make sense, then, if the market is moving higher that you should buy stocks. Otherwise, if the market is moving lower, you should not buy stocks. During this time,

you should be in cash or a Bearish strategy. Good examples of Bearish strategies are shorting stocks or buying put options.

Figure 2.1. Log into the Market Trend Signal Web site to find MTS indicators.

Market Trend Signal™ defines the market as the S&P 500. I know there are a million definitions of what the market is—that just adds to the confusion. There is no magic to what makes up the market, folks. MTS™ evaluates five hundred stocks for its main signal, which is a big enough sample size. To make it even simpler, MTS™ also uses SPY which is the iShare ETF (Exchange Traded Fund) used to create trend calculations.

ST Trend and SPY Rating

Market Trend Signal™ is made up of two parts: the ST trend of SPY and the rating of SPY. There are two main categories of trend and four sub-categories of market conditions. The two main categories of trend are Bull market and Bear market. A Bull market is defined as SPY moving higher within approximately a 180 day (six months) time frame and vice-versa for a Bear market.

Within Bull and Bear markets are smaller degrees of trend or market conditions. These sub-category conditions are: *Bullish, Mild Bull, Mild Bear* and *Bearish*. When ST trend is UP and there is a BUY rating on SPY, the Market Trend Signal™ is Bullish. If the signal has a Bull market reading, it provides the absolute best trading environment to buy stocks. If, on the other hand, the signal is Bearish in a Bear market, these are conditions where stocks will not perform well. If you find yourself in a Bearish/Bear market, you should be in cash or other Bearish strategies.

Trading conditions can be good in a Bullish MTS™ environment, but the risk of false signals is much higher. The first step in the trading process is identifying the market trend. You must identify what direction the market is going. Market Trend Signal™ gives you this information.

Step Two: StrengthRank™ to Find Leadership

StrengthRank™ is a calculation of a stock's performance versus a small universe of stocks (about 8,000). High rankings show that a stock is performing well. For example, a 98 ranking signifies that a stock is currently outperforming 98% of all other stocks. A ranking of five signifies the stock is underperforming 95% of all other stocks. These ranks allow you to know quickly if the stock is showing strength or not. Our system separates stock rankings and ETF rankings.

Exchange Traded Fund (ETF) rankings are in relation to other ETFs (not other stocks), so you're given clear performance rankings of ETFs relative to their peers. Many stocks that have moved fifty to 100% and have climbed to high rankings over 90 are often just getting started in their trending moves. You may be following a stock that has gone from the 90s to the 70s in a matter of days. This is a good warning sign, as there may be reasons why the stock is losing steam and may be getting ready to shift trends.

This, in addition to a ST trend down, or a move from BUY to HOLD, may solidify your action to sell the stock. Stocks breaking out to new highs with high rankings will perform amazingly well in Bullish/Bull market conditions on the Market Trend Signal™. In Bear market environments, however, these stocks can sometimes be punished quickly if they show any waver in price or trend whatsoever.

The goal of MTS™ is to find stocks that become strong and stay strong. Stocks priced under five dollars are not included in the rankings and will display as 'Not Ranked.' The kind of stocks that MTS™ qualifies as high-ranking are those that have often started out by gaining a hundred percent, move to 200% then, in some cases, gain thousands of percentage points before the trend turns. Stocks like HANS and TASR which produced one thousand percent to 4000% return in the last 2003-2007 Bull market are used as our examples.

U TRENDS UNIVERSITY

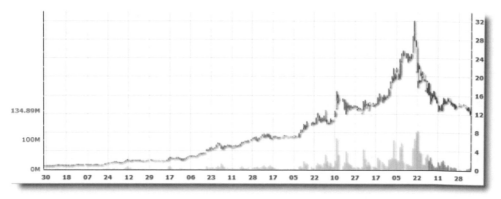

Figure 2.2. TASER International Inc (TASR) trade statistics from 06/01/03 through 06/20/04.

Figure 2.3. TASER International Inc (TASR) chart from 06/01/03 through 06/20/04.

Using a long only strategy, TASER International Inc (TASR) gained over 1200% in one year (*see* Figures 2.2 and 2.3). An investment of ten thousand dollars would have turned into $120,000.

During that exact time frame, another stock, Hansen Natural Corp (HANS) which is the maker of fruit drinks and Monster™ energy drinks catapulted to its highest peak, making many investors very wealthy. Again, a ten thousand dollar investment increased in value to $390,000 in one year (*see* Figures 2.4 and 2.5). This stock ended up gaining over 7000% when the trend ended.

Figure 2.4. Hansen Natural Corp (HANS) trade statistics from 06/01/03 through 06/20/04.

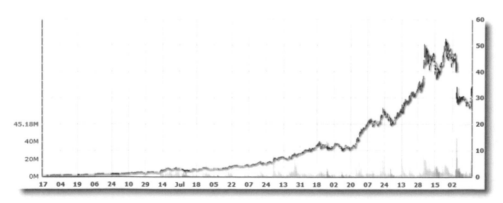

Figure 2.5. Hansen Natural Corp (HANS) trade chart from 06/01/03 through 06/20/04.

Step Three: Stock Direction

Warren Buffett and Ben Graham gave birth to "value" investing by studiously spending hours upon hours digging and sifting through piles of paperwork to find that nugget— that little golden "ah-ha" nugget—and that's because value investing actually does work. Yes, for some like Buffet, uncovering every last valuation "fundamental" does work for a group of investors called "institutional investors" because institutional investors already have billions of dollars to throw around. They may also have five Harvard grads with their noses in every financial document a company may have, and they are bound to uncover something that determines a possible gold mine.

For you, all that information *is* irrelevant. For you and me, it's about being rich, not about being smart or being right. Remember the commentary in chapter 1? We said that institutions move markets and make trends—not you and not me. Therefore, we will follow the lead and the lead is *always* price movement. I'm not completely against knowing things about the companies of the stocks I trade, like what they do and how they do it. I am a business junky and I do like to find out more details about a company, but that information *never* goes into buy or sell decisions.

After determining that market conditions are Bullish, you'll want to find and trade stocks with high StrengthRank™ ratings. You'll find stocks that are trending higher and that are already proving themselves. There are several tools MTS™ offers. The first one we'll look at is the Stock Screener.

Stock Screener Basics

There are two parts to the Stock Screener: the Input tab and the Results tab. The Input tab allows you to define how narrow of a screen to submit (*see* Figure 2.6). The default settings are: 'All' which is selected in the 'Industry' column; a share price of five dollars or greater; ratings set to 'BUY'; and StrengthRank™ of 95 or better. The results of these criteria will give you a listing of stocks that are the cream of the crop as far as MTS™ is concerned. They are trending UP and they're outperforming 95% of all other stocks. Once criteria are selected, click on 'Find Stocks' at the bottom of the page.

Figure 2.6. Find Stocks criteria input page.

As I write this, market conditions are quite Bullish, so there are a lot of stocks showing up in the results area…72 to be exact. This system is capped at 201 displayed results. MTS™ determines that you don't need any more than that, because there's really no point to list any others. With such a large number of stocks, you can begin to narrow down your search using other screening criteria.

Let's narrow down the search by adding volume criteria. We'll only look for stocks that are trading a twenty day average of five million shares. I've checked the 'Volume' box and selected the 'Min: 5 mil' option.

Market Trend Signal™
Market Timing - Trend Following - Stock Ratings

Chapter 2: What is Market Trend Signal™?

Figure 2.7. Search form criteria on the Find Stocks input page.

UTRENDS UNIVERSITY

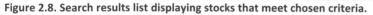

Symbol	Name	Last	ST Trend	Rating	Strength Rank
RDN	Radian Group Inc	13.4000	Up	Buy	98
GNW	Genworth Finl Inc	17.1600	Up	Buy	97
FITB	Fifth Third Bancorp	13.6300	Up	Buy	97
LVS	Las Vegas Sands Corp	21.2400	Up	Buy	97
DDR	Developers Diversified Rlty	12.5500	Up	Buy	95
F	Ford Mtr Co Del	13.9200	Up	Buy	95

Figure 2.8. Search results list displaying stocks that meet chosen criteria.

Adding volume criteria reduces the results to six—a much more manageable list of stocks to choose from. The results page offers an export function at the bottom of the page, so you can save your results to spread sheets for quick reference. The Stock Screener also offers access to symbols for analysis in other areas of the program. Clicking on any of the symbols will take you to the 'Stock Analysis' page were you can view a chart, news, options, back test, and other details of the stock.

Stock Screener Strategies

The Stock Screener is designed to give you many strategy tools. We will cover a couple here and several more in the following three chapters. A strategy (in addition to the one I just pointed out) is looking for stocks which have gone from a Hold rating to a Buy rating.

Keeping the criteria the same as the previous example, let's reduce the volume to '500 k', instead of five million, and add the Rating Change: HOLD to BUY. Click on the radio button to select 'Rating Change' in the Ratings section. You can choose criteria combinations by clicking on their dropdown lists.

Stock Screener	Search Results : 2				Back To Screener	
Symbol	Name	Last	ST Trend	Rating	Strength Rank
VCI	Valassis Communications Inc	28.6000	Up	Buy	98
AGO	Assured Guaranty Ltd	21.8300	Up	Buy	95

Figure 2.9. Search Results page showing 2 candidates found from the screen criteria entered.

The results page gives you two stocks ready to trade now! This is the beauty of this screen. Market conditions are Bullish (I know because MTS™ shows me it is). Because of the market conditions, I want to trade high ranking stocks and I want to trade stocks that are just beginning the trend or just breaking out to advance an existing trend.

Figure 2.10. Valassis Communications Inc (VCI) showing a BUY rating on the Stock Analysis chart page.

In Figure 2.10, we have chosen Valassis Communications Inc (VCI) as our example. Click on the VCI row to select it. The 'Stock Analysis' page displays the VCI chart, showing the stock in a clear UP trend that is ready to break out of the current price high of $29—a perfect trade set up! LT and ST trends are UP and the StrengthRank™ is 98, which means it's a leader in this rally. The rating has just changed from HOLD to BUY...giddeeup!

To finish this step, we need to check the back-tested performance of the stock. Some stocks trend better than others and react to the MTS™ system better than others. A very choppy stock will give many false Buy and Sell signals, resulting in "whipsaw."

Whipsaw is one drawback to any trading method. It simply means that once a signal is given, the stock immediately reverses (goes in the other direction) and you're forced to exit the trade. Whipsawing often happens at market tops and bottoms, and is the cost

of trading. Once the trend starts or resumes, losses incurred from a whipsaw event are quickly recovered.

Think of trading like it's a business. In all businesses, there are costs or expenses that must be incurred to make a profit. In trading, one of your costs *is* your losses. Losses are not fun, but they are required. You are "required" to follow the rules of the trading system, and you are required to rely on the probability of success. Think of it as two steps forward and one step back. It may start out as one step back then two steps forward. Whatever the order, it is simply a part of the trading process and should not be feared.

To get a better sense of how this stock reacts to the MTS™ trading system, a longer sample time frame of back testing is needed. If I move the start date all the way back to January 1, 2000, the VCI stock shows the results in Figure 2.11.

Back Test	Equity Curve		StockSymbol	VCI			
Trade Stats for	**VCI**		Current Signal	Buy		Please select buy/sell criteria	
Number of Trades	34	Trade expectancy	$3464.29	☑ Long			
Total Profit amount	$219,823.47	Trade expectancy%	34.64%	Buy		Sell	
Total Loss amount	$21,759.55	Annual Trade expectancy	$12,392.11	Buy ▾		Sell ▾	
Total Profit or Total Loss	$198,063.92	Annual Trade expectancy%	123.92%				
Avg Profit on Winners	$12,930.79	Largest profit	$130,390.81	☐ Short			
Avg Loss on Losers	$1,279.97	Largest loss	$6,931.54	Sell		Buy	
Total Net % gain or loss	1980.64%	Avg days in trade	51	Buy ▾		Sell ▾	
Aver % gain on Winners	76.84%	Avg days between trades	49				
Aver % loss on Losers	7.56%						
Reward to Risk Ratio	10.17			Investment dollars:		10000	
Number of Trades Per year	3.6						
Number of Winners	17			Additions on Signals			
Number of Losers	17			☑ Compound original invesment			
Winning Percentage	50.00			☐ Use fixed amount on new signal			
Start date	09/26/2000	End date	03/25/2010			Query	

Figure 2.11. Valassis Communications Inc (VCI) back test results used for back test showing trades from 09/26/2000 through 03/25/2010.

In Figure 2.11, MTS™ gave thirty-four trades on VCI stock over a period of 9 years. This works out to seventeen winners and 17 losers with an average gain of 76.84% per trade.

The average loss was nearly eight percent per trade. Therefore, the winning percentage on this stock has been 50%. This is not bad, as long as there is at least a three to one reward to risk (3:1). The reward to risk is 10.17 (76.84%/-7.56%), meaning that you are making almost ten times as much on your winners as you are losing on your losers. This stock has a per-trade expectancy of 34.64%, making it an amazing candidate to trade. Additional screener strategies are found in *Chapter 3: Identifying High Probability Trades using Market Trend Signal™* and on our DVD trainings at www.TrendsUniversity.com

Step Four: Money Management

The fourth step in the MTS™ trading system is money management—the single most important aspect of trading. Without proper money management, even the most successful trading methodology can lose money.

In *Chapter 5: Money Management*, we'll give you a clearer understanding for how to choose a market and how to determine entry and exit timing using various money management tools for evaluating stocks and ETFs inside the MTS™ system. We'll also touch on trade expectancy, how to balance long and short positions, and how to deal with market drawdown.

Step Five: Trade Decision

Step five in the MTS™ trading system is about making wise trade decisions. The decision-making process holds fundamental keys to a trader's success. Our goal is to ensure that you are equipped with knowledge that will not only limit your losses, but also increase your gains using the MTS™ system.

In *Chapter 4: Decision and Trade Management*, we'll cover essential trading strategies and formulas you can use to prepare entry and exit timing with precision. Topics include how to avoid typical emotional cycles, trading on margin, and how to gain resolve in Bearish markets.

Step Six: Trade Management

Step six in the MTS™ trading system is about managing trades. In *Chapter 4: Decision and Trade Management*, we'll cover order types that can be placed to ensure success for your trades. We'll also give you strategies for how to use these order types, determining and placing pre-determined limits such as stop and limit with your broker, trading on margin, and the art of shorting stocks.

Back Testing / Trade Expectancy & Probabilities

When you back test a stock, a report is generated in the MTS™ 'Backtest' tab which shows you critical statistical data. These results give you an informed perspective on how a stock trades within the MTS™ system. Back testing can also be done to research a stock's history and to gather information about trading conditions that may have affected a stock's performance in the past.

The definition of trade expectancy varies by system. In the case of MTS™, trade expectancy is defined as: trade expectancy = (probability of win * average win) – (probability of loss * average loss). If the calculation returns a positive number, a trader will make money over time. MTS™ uses probability of success scenarios for any given stock based on back testing results.

Trade expectancy includes both winners and losers, so it is a fair look at how the overall performance has been on a stock. Trade expectancy is displayed as a percentage. The MTS™ back test displays the dollar value, percentage, annual trade expectancy, and annual percent. On average, most stocks have about three trades per year, so the annual expectancy is the trade expectancy percentage multiplied by the number of trades per year.

To back test, click on the 'Analysis Tools' to open the 'Market Indexes' page, then click on the 'Backtest' tab and enter the symbol of the stock you want to investigate into the 'StockSymbol' box (*see* Figure 2.12). Default search criteria are set to the current year, with a 'Long' only, 'Buy' and 'Sell'. A (default setting) search result will return statistics

beginning on the default start date through the current date. You have the option to change default 'Buy' and 'Sell' criteria by clicking on their dropdown list.

You can also access the back test function from the 'Stock Analysis' page. Enter the stock you're researching into the 'Symbol' box and determine the date span of the chart you want to view by clicking the radio buttons. Note that a six month time frame is the default chart view. From here, you can click on the 'Backtest' button next to the 'Symbol' box which will take you to the 'Backtest' page, populate the forms, and run the back test automatically. The test will run the same time frame as you selected for the chart view, i.e. 'By Calendar,' or specific time frames: '3 mo,' '6 mo,' '1 yr,' or '2yrs'

Back Test	**Equity Curve**	StockSymbol

Trade Stats for	**BZH**	Current Signal	Buy
Number of Trades	34	Trade expectancy	$1153.61
Total Profit amount	$262,122.94	Trade expectancy%	11.53%
Total Loss amount	$125,543.05	Annual Trade expectancy	$3,834.06
Total Profit or Total Loss	$136,579.88	Annual Trade expectancy%	38.34%
Avg Profit on Winners	$13,795.94	Largest profit	$105,311.45
Avg Loss on Losers	$8,369.54	Largest loss	$39,839.22
Total Net % gain or loss	1365.80%		
Aver % gain on Winners	28.94%		
Aver % loss on Losers	10.51%		
Reward to Risk Ratio	2.75		
Number of Trades Per year	3.3		
Number of Winners	19		
Number of Losers	15		
Winning Percentage	55.88		

Please select buy/sell criteria

☑ Long

Buy — Sell

Buy ▾   Sell ▾

☐ Short

Sell — Buy

Buy ▾   Sell ▾

Investment dollars: 10000

Additions on Signals

☑ Compound original invesment
☐ Use fixed amount on new signal

Start date 01/01/2000   End date 03/23/2010

Query

Figure 2.12. Back test of BZH showing a 10 year trade expectancy of 11.53% per trade and 38.34% per year for 10 years.

The statistics page for the back test presents you with all the data you will need to go forward with a high level of confidence in each trade. The first thing to look for is the 'Annual Trade expectancy %,' which will give you a quick glance at the kind of performance you could expect from a stock. Granted, I will give you all the same disclaimers about past performance not being an indication of future performance, but I will add that it statistically remains to be the best indication of future performance within the MTS™ system.

Market Trend Signal™

Market Timing - Trend Following - Stock Ratings

The MTS™ system presents you with performance statistics, giving you an edge in your trading decisions. Statistical probabilities are covered more thoroughly in *Chapter 5: Money Management*.

To fully consider the probability of a trade, you need more data. Pulling samples from the past decade provides enough time and circumstance to have a good feel of how stocks will react to the system. How far back do we need to test? The MTS™ system allows for researching as much as twelve years of statistical information, which ensures that the highs and lows of market extremes are included in evaluation results. For example, over the past ten years, we have experienced two historical Bull markets and two historical Bear markets. These unprecedented market shifts provide deep data analysis coverage of market conditions within the MTS™ framework.

In Figures 2.13 and 2.14, the chart of Advanced Micro Devices Inc (AMD) shows an expectancy of 43.59% annual gain. Every winner gained 46.18% on average, and just over ten percent loss on every loser. You could expect to make four trades per year and win forty percent of the time, with a reward to risk ratio of 4.3:1.

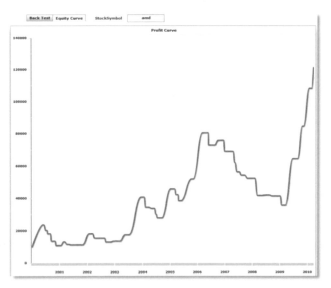

Figure 2.13. Advanced Micro Devices Inc (AMD) equity curve showing high expectancy.

Back Test	Equity Curve	StockSymbol	amd

Trade Stats for	**AMD**		Current Signal	Buy
Number of Trades	38	Trade expectancy	$1173.69
Total Profit amount	$199,204.80	Trade expectancy%	11.73%
Total Loss amount	$87,749.70	Annual Trade expectancy	$4,359.46
Total Profit or Total Loss	$111,455.09	Annual Trade expectancy%	43.59%
Avg Profit on Winners	$13,280.32	Largest profit	$28,623.32
Avg Loss on Losers	$3,815.20	Largest loss	$10,604.59
Total Net % gain or loss	1114.55%	Avg days in trade	47
Aver % gain on Winners	46.18%	Avg days between trades	53
Aver % loss on Losers	10.73%	Longest nbr of consecutive winners	
Reward to Risk Ratio	4.31	Longest nbr of consecutive losers	
Number of Trades Per year	3.7	Largest Drawdown	
Number of Winners	15	Avg Drawdown	
Number of Losers	23		
Winning Percentage	39.47		

Please select buy/sell criteria

☑ Long

Buy   Sell

| Buy ▾ | Sell ▾ |

☐ Short

Sell   Buy

| Sell ▾ | Buy ▾ |

Investment dollars: 10000

Additions on Signals

☑ Compound original invesment
☐ Use fixed amount on new signal

Start date 01/01/2000   End date 03/23/2010

Query

Figure 2.14. Historical trade statistics for Advanced Micro Devices Inc (AMD) long only trades from 01/01/2000 through 03/23/2010.

TRENDS UNIVERSITY

Back Test	Equity Curve		StockSymbol	amd	

Trade Stats for	**AMD**		Current Signal	Buy	
Number of Trades	75	Trade expectancy	$838.16	
Total Profit amount	$654,761.66	Trade expectancy%	8.38%	
Total Loss amount	$294,184.69	Annual Trade expectancy	$6,146.91	
Total Profit or Total Loss	$360,576.97	Annual Trade expectancy%	61.47%	
Avg Profit on Winners	$19,841.26	Largest profit	$109,214.38	
Avg Loss on Losers	$7,004.40	Largest loss	$50,131.19	
Total Net % gain or loss	3605.77%	Avg days in trade	0	
Aver % gain on Winners	32.47%	Avg days between trades	0	
Aver % loss on Losers	10.54%	Longest nbr of consecutive winners		
Reward to Risk Ratio	3.08	Longest nbr of consecutive losers		
Number of Trades Per year	7.3	Largest Drawdown		
Number of Winners	33	Avg Drawdown		
Number of Losers	42			
Winning Percentage	44.00			

Please select buy/sell criteria

☑ Long

Buy — Sell

Buy ▾   Sell ▾

☑ Short

Sell — Buy

Sell ▾   Buy ▾

Investment dollars: 10000

Additions on Signals

☑ Compound original invesment

☐ Use fixed amount on new signal

Start date 01/01/2000   End date 03/23/2010

Query

Figure 2.15. Historical trade statistics for Advanced Micro Devices Inc (AMD) from 01/01/2000 through 03/23/2010.

Trading AMD on a long/short basis starting at the beginning of 2000 through November 4, 2009 would have pocketed you 3,605% over the past ten years. This is the kind of information you want to know about a stock and about a system before going into the trade. It only takes a few minutes to determine if certain stocks trade well within the MTS™ system. If the expectancy or reward risk is not within your trading plan, move on to a better expectancy on another stock.

Trade expectancy allows a trader to quickly determine if a stock trades well within the MTS™ system. Not all stocks will have great performance statics, but the ones that do are key candidates to continue to trade repeatedly in your trading account. Trade expectancy is covered in more detail in *Chapter 4: Decision and Trade Management*.

Stock Analysis

The Stock Analysis page is broken into four pages: *Quote, News, Chart* and *Option Chain*. In this section, we will take a closer look at the functionality of the chart page.

TRENDS UNIVERSITY

The Chart Page

The default landing page for the Stock Analysis link is called the "chart" or "main" page (*see* Figure 2.16). MTS™ uses candlestick charts that are colored according to the stock's rating for that date. The coloring will be green, yellow or red to correspond with the BUY, HOLD or SELL ratings, respectively. The chart page also displays volume bars which are color-coded to the corresponding rating. This visual aid not only allows you to quickly glance at the history of the stock to see how it has performed after a rating has been given, but also helps you to quickly determine when the last rating change took place.

Figure 2.16. Example of typical stock analysis chart page showing Microsoft Corp (MSFT) data.

Look at the graphic in Figure 2.16. Above the chart, you will notice the date radio buttons and the signal buttons. You can click on the ST trend or LT trend of the stock to

have their current and historical signals show up on the chart. The default chart setting is a six month snapshot. You can change the chart view to three months, one year, two years, or you have the option to create a custom time frame view. The slider bar at the bottom of the chart will allow you to *slide* the chart into a custom view.

Notes and Comments

Market Trend Signal™

Market Timing - Trend Following - Stock Ratings

Notes and Comments

Chapter 3
Identifying High Probability Trades using Market Trend Signal™

Contents

MuscleStocks are not only specific kinds of stocks we are looking to trade, they are also the name of a group of predefined screens on the MTS™ system. These screen types also include *Smooth Sailin*, *New Buys*, *Muscle Minis*, *Muscle Break Outs*, *Weaklings*, *Spring Loaded*, and *Bottoms UP*. In this chapter, I will explain these and what each one offers.

MuscleStocks

All *MuscleStocks* are Buy rated stocks whose price is greater than five dollars with a StrengthRank™ of 98 and an average volume of at least two hundred thousand. These stocks are the cream of the crop in the MTS™ system.

These stocks are trending upward and out performing 98% of all other stocks. When market conditions are Bullish in a Bull market, these stocks will sing. Take for example, the current list of stocks on the screen as I make this update.

Market Indexes	Sectors	Stock Analysis	Backtest	Stock Screener	Portfolio	Watch List	MuscleStocks	MuscleETF's

MuscleStocks	Smooth Sailin	New Buys	Muscle Minis	Muscle Break Outs	Spring Loaded	Bottoms Up	Weaklings	Sell to Buy

	Symbol	Name	Last	ST Trend	Rating	Strength Rank
⊙	JAZZ	Jazz Pharmaceuticals Inc	12.3300	Down	Buy	98
⊙	ARM	Arvinmeritor Inc	13.4600	Up	Buy	98
⊙	AXL	American Axle & Mfg Hldgs In	10.5200	Down	Buy	98
⊙	ZOOM	Zoom Tech Inc	7.7200	Up	Buy	98
⊙	BZ	Boise Inc	5.9000	Up	Buy	98
⊙	WNC	Wabash Natl Corp	7.4400	Up	Buy	98
⊙	VNDA	Vanda Pharmaceuticals Inc	11.7600	Down	Buy	98
⊙	CHRS	Charming Shoppes	6.6300	Down	Buy	98
⊙	CIT	Cit Group Inc	39.0100	Up	Buy	98
⊙	VCI	Valassis Communications Inc	28.3200	Down	Buy	98
⊙	SRZ	Sunrise Senior Living Inc	5.3500	Down	Buy	98
⊙	DAN	Dana Holding Corp	12.4800	Up	Buy	98
⊙	DNDN	Dendreon Cp	36.6100	Up	Buy	98

MuscleStocks are BUY Rated stocks whose price is greater than $5, Rank is 98 with average volume of at least 200,000   Export To .CSV

Figure 3.1. *MuscleStocks* search results list.

The MTS™ system displays several Buy rated stocks from which to choose. Let's look at two of the listings shown in Figure 3.1: COT and ETM. We'll also include TASR (not shown) in our examples. All of these stocks are what we consider *MuscleStocks* because their price is greater than five dollars with a StrengthRank™ of 98 and an average volume of at least two hundred thousand.

TRENDS
UNIVERSITY

In chapter 2, we used TASER International Inc (TASR) to show you the performance of the stock about six months into the new Bull market of 2003. In a matter of a few months, the stock's value increased 300%. Most investors would be intimidated and shy away from buying this kind of stock because of the huge percentage gain it had experienced. As an MTS™ trader, you have the tools to invest in these kinds of stocks with confidence.

In Figure 3.2, TASR was only at the beginning of an upward trend. The stock continued to rise and gained another 500% before it finally made a significant correction.

Figure 3.2. TASER International Inc (TASR) chart from 04/14/2003 through 10/14/2003.

TRENDS
UNIVERSITY

Figure 3.3. TASER International Inc (TASR) chart from 10/14/2003 through 04/23/2004.

The power of trend following stocks is shown in Figures 3.2 and 3.3. As we see with TASR, it is possible for a stock to continue on an upward trend to surprising heights, and at times, can climb to *unimaginable* levels. Many traders sell out too soon or are afraid to get back in when this occurs. Remember, if market conditions are Bullish, then buying high StrengthRank™ stocks with Buy ratings are very high probability trades.

Now, look at Boise Inc (BZ)—a *MuscleStock* found in month twelve of the new '09 Bull market (*see* Figure 3.4).

U TRENDS NIVERSITY

Figure 3.4. Boise, Inc (BZ) chart from 04/04/2008 through 03/25/2010.

Figure 3.5. Boise, Inc (BZ) performance statistics from 02/04/2009 through 03/25/2010.

In Figure 3.5, BZ shows gains over 800% on four trades over the course of thirteen months, starting in February of 2009 and ending in March of 2010. What ever the reason, the stock is performing amazingly well. Could it be earnings? Probably. Could it

be expected earnings? Possibly. Could it be new market share or profit margins or maybe cost-cutting or a new product mix? Whatever is the reason, *who cares*? It doesn't matter a bit! Does knowing why the stock is moving up really do anything for you? Does it help in the BUY or SELL process? I argue that it doesn't help because the stock will usually rise on rumor versus news anyway.

Keep in mind that information known or anticipated is already showing in the price. The stock is trending higher and the probability of it continuing to do so is good in Bullish market conditions.

You may certainly spend hours of your valuable time reading up on a target company, digging and poking—prodding at whatever information you might find interesting, but those activities amount to hours wasted. You could be playing with the kids or visiting with the spouse, exercising, or enjoying your favorite George Winston music—all my favorite pastimes.

The point here is that the stock is trending and doing so with vigor. Listen to what the market is telling you until the market stops trending. When it stops, you'll have a clear SELL signal to let you know it's time to lock in gains and move on to the next stock.

Take Entercom Communications Corp (ETM) which is a similar situation. In Figures 3.6 and 3.7, the stock has been in the *MuscleStock* screen since the $6 breakout. There is still huge potential for the stock, until there isn't. You may be raising an eyebrow at that last statement. Let me repeat myself: There is still huge potential for the stock, until there *isn't*. What I mean by this is the trend is currently working and nothing (yet) is telling you that it should not continue to work. What you *don't* want to do is get married to this stock—looking and hoping that it will be your ticket to retirement. Trade the trend until it no longer works. The signal for selling is a big fat *red* SELL!

U TRENDS
HIVERSITY

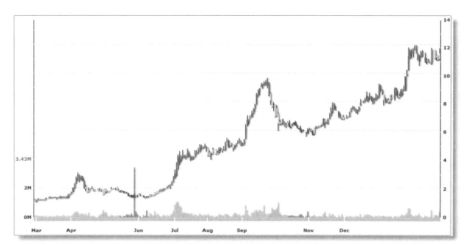

Figure 3.6. Entercom Communications Corp (ETM) chart from 3/01/2009 through 03/25/2010.

| Back Test | Equity Curve | StockSymbol | etm |

Trade Stats for ETM — Current Signal: Buy — Please select buy/sell criteria

Number of Trades	3	Trade expectancy	0	☑ Long
Total Profit amount	$76,881.74	Trade expectancy%	101.84%	
Total Loss amount	0	Annual Trade expectancy	$35,741.92	Buy — Sell
Total Profit or Total Loss	$76,881.74	Annual Trade expectancy%	357.42%	Buy ▾ Sell ▾
Avg Profit on Winners	$25,627.25	Largest profit	$38,000.93	
Avg Loss on Losers	0	Largest loss	0	☐ Short
Total Net % gain or loss	768.82%	Avg days in trade	92	Sell — Buy
Aver % gain on Winners	121.88%	Avg days between trades	33	Buy ▾ Sell ▾
Aver % loss on Losers	0			
Reward to Risk Ratio	0			
Number of Trades Per year	3.0			Investment dollars: 10000
Number of Winners	3			Additions on Signals
Number of Losers	0			☑ Compound original invesment
Winning Percentage	100%			☐ Use fixed amount on new signal

Start date 03/30/2009   End date 03/25/2010   Query

Figure 3.7. Entercom Communications Corp (ETM) performance statistics from 3/30/2009 through 03/25/2010.

Smooth Sailin

Smooth Sailin provides a list of stocks that are Buy rated, ten dollars or greater with a StrengthRank™ of 90 or greater and have an average volume of one million or greater. These stocks also all have options trading on them.

TRW Automotive Holdings Corp (TRW), for example, has been a great performing stock during the 2009 rally. The stock showed up in scans in early June (*see* Figure 3.8) and increased its value over 100% in a little over a month. Again on November 4, the stock was added to the *Smooth Sailin* scan, as it met the criteria of the scan moving from HOLD to BUY. It went on to gain over 22% in four trading days. These kinds of stocks are followed by institutions: volume is high, and they are worth looking at every day. Some of these stocks will make you thirty to 100% profit in a matter of a few weeks when conditions are Bullish.

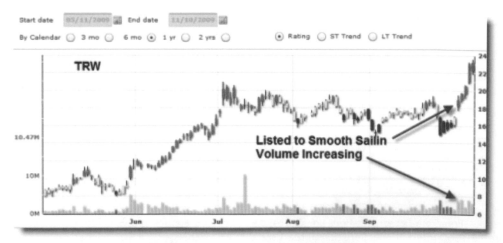

Figure 3.8. TRW Automotive Holdings Corp (TRW) chart from 5/11/2009 through 11/10/2009.

New Buys

New Buys will find stocks whose price is five dollars or greater and have had a Hold rating on the previous day which has changed to a Buy rating. *New Buys* finds StrengthRank™ stocks of 90 or greater with an average volume of 100,000 or greater.

Do you feel like you waste hours each day looking for just the right trade? Do you watch financial news channels and wait for something that looks like a useful tidbit of information so you can jump on the "hot" stock? That is truly a waste of time. The *New Buys* screen gives you stocks making moves now! The foundation is already in place because the stocks it finds are high StrengthRank™ with *New Buys* ratings. The program gives an amazing list of stocks to choose from. It's like, "shooting fish in a barrel," so they say.

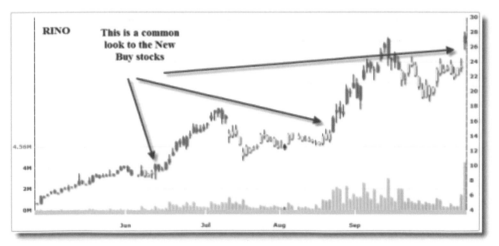

Figure 3.9. RINO International Corp (RINO) chart showing BUY signals after a HOLD signal.

Muscle Minis

Muscle Minis finds stocks whose prices are between one and five dollars. The stocks have had a rating change from HOLD to BUY in the past day. The average volume on

these stocks is 500,000 per day or greater. These are stocks that have the potential to *pop*. In early stage Bull markets these stocks get gobbled up like hot cakes and can rocket from 300% to as much as six hundred percent.

The risk is obviously higher and the volatility can be intense. These are stocks you do *not* touch in Bearish market conditions. The high risk flag is there because these stocks are usually cheap for a reason. For example, a company's fundamentals may be breaking down, and so on. It doesn't matter the reason they are going down in a Bear market. In Bull markets, they are there for the "pickins."

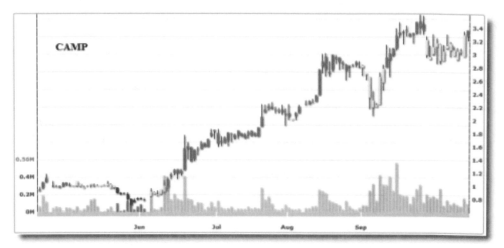

Figure 3.10. CalAmp Corp (CAMP) chart showing strong returns in Bullish market conditions.

Muscle Break Outs

Muscle Break Outs finds stocks with a price of five dollars or greater with a StrengthRank™ of 80 or greater. These stocks have had a rating change from HOLD to BUY and the current day's volume is 80% greater from that of the previous day. The average five-day volume is 100,000 or greater. Big volume means institutional money is entering the stock.

Figure 3.11. Smart Modular Technologies Inc. (SMOD). HOLD to BUY on 80% volume increase from the previous day.

Back Test	Equity Curve	StockSymbol	SMOD

Trade Stats for **SMOD**   Current Signal   Buy

Please select buy/sell criteria

Number of Trades	4	Trade expectancy	0
Total Profit amount	$24,541.82	Trade expectancy%	17.77%
Total Loss amount	0	Annual Trade expectancy	$4,780.87
Total Profit or Total Loss	$24,541.82	Annual Trade expectancy%	47.81%
Avg Profit on Winners	$6,135.46	Largest profit	$8,000.00
Avg Loss on Losers	0	Largest loss	0
Total Net % gain or loss	245.42%	Avg days in trade	91
Aver % gain on Winners	38.87%	Avg days between trades	31
Aver % loss on Losers	0		
Reward to Risk Ratio	0		
Number of Trades Per year	3.8		
Number of Winners	4		
Number of Losers	0		
Winning Percentage	100%		

☑ Long

Buy   Sell

Buy ▾	Sell ▾

☐ Short

Sell   Buy

Buy ▾	Sell ▾

Investment dollars: 10000

Additions on Signals

☑ Compound original invesment
☐ Use fixed amount on new signal

Start date   03/01/2009   End date   03/25/2010

Query

Figure 3.12. Smart Modular Technologies Inc. (SMOD) performance statistics from 03/01/2009 through 03/25/2010.

In Figure 3.11, Smart Modular Technologies Inc. (SMOD) shows that taking the HOLD to BUY trade while on big volume has been quite profitable over a twelve month time frame. Note that this price action leads stocks higher and increases the probability of a successful trade (*see* Figure 3.12).

Weaklings

Weaklings finds stocks with prices five dollars or greater where StrengthRank™ is 50 or lower and when stocks have gone from HOLD to SELL. Volume, in this case, is twenty percent greater on the current day over the previous day.

These stocks are simply just not cutting it, in most cases. They are under performing compared to 50% or more of the universe of stocks and they are trending downward. In Bearish market conditions, these stocks are the place to look for shorting opportunities. They are often just heading to the cliff before taking that final plunge.

In Bullish market conditions, however, you need to be cautious of shorting these stocks heavily. Shorting weak stocks in a strong market is not the highest probability trade for those circumstances. Just because the scans are there doesn't mean we will use them all the time. Some of the scans will have more relevance in Bull markets while others, like *Weaklings*, will be more relevant in Bear markets.

The stock in this example has recently made the *Weakling* list. Now, there are many things that could or "should" happen once a signal is given, but the bottom line is: who knows what's going to happen? We take a trade based on statistics and use sound money management techniques.

In Figure 3.13, notice that current market conditions are Bullish. Taking on any large position in a Bearish strategy doesn't make much sense.

U TRENDS UNIVERSITY

Stock could venture here

Figure 3.13. Stocks often continue to trend lower after a Sell signal. The red callout box points to the probable location of the continued downward trend.

Spring Loaded

Spring Loaded finds stocks with prices greater than five dollars that are Hold rated with a StrengthRank™ of 80 or greater and where the ST trend has gone from DN (down) to UP in the past day. The average volume on these stocks is 20,000 or greater.

The *Spring Loaded* screen program is a very powerful tool to find stocks that may be very early in the trend. The ST trend signal gives you confirmation of the trend within one or two days of a bottom. The Hold rating will offer a higher probability that the bottom is close but also can get you into a trade five to 8% before a Buy signal is given.

Figure 3.14. Avis Budget Group Inc (CAR) performance chart showing movement from a Sell rating to a Hold rating. The stock is in a position to continue an upward trend.

Bottoms UP

Bottoms UP finds stocks with a price of five dollars or greater with a StrengthRank™ of less than 50 where ratings have gone from HOLD to BUY in the past day. The average five-day volume is 200,000 or greater.

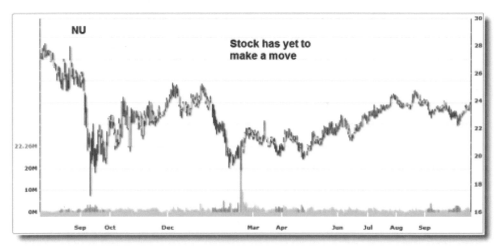

Figure 3.15. Northeast Utilities (NU) performance chart showing it's in a range to continue an upward trend.

Market Trend Signal™ Helps to Prevent Common Investor Mistakes

Many traders buy on the way down, hoping for the stock to rise—this is called "dollar cost" averaging. Dollar cost averaging is a method used to buy stock when it is trending down in price, rather than making the purchase when a stock is trending upward.

I mentioned in chapter 1 that this method of trading is *garbage* trading. Some super long-term institutional investors may be able to get away with it, but you probably don't have the time or the money to mess with their strategy. The biggest mistake is locking up your capital while waiting for it to make you money. It's craziness! You should be buying stocks that have the potential to start making you money immediately. MTS™ will not allow you to buy on the way down.

Often, traders buy large amounts of low priced stocks rather than smaller amounts of higher priced stocks. Higher priced stocks are often stocks that are working and trending higher. As with most products, you often get what you pay for. Stocks are no different. If you buy a cheap penny stock, you're buying a stock with underlying business issues. If the business was running well or expected to run well in the near future, the stock

would not be so cheap. Stocks with big price tags can mean just the opposite: the business is firing on all cylinders and investors are willing to pay up for it. MTS™ will find stocks trending higher. Signals can still be given on low priced stocks but StrengthRank™ will tell you the power behind the trend. High StrengthRank™ stocks will find strong or expected-to-be strong business.

Wanting to Make a Quick Buck and Get Rich Quickly

We prefer using the saying "get rich slowly." Have you honestly ever heard of a "get rich quick" idea that benefited anyone other than the person selling it? If you're thinking, 'no,' I agree with you, because I haven't either. I want you to get rich in a sustainable fashion—in a way that can truly benefit your life without sending you on a financial roller-coaster.

The term "slow" (to me) is not thirty years. "Slow" is three to 7 years, not the next six months. I'm still talking about making significant gains in a time frame that you can actually enjoy life with the funds...not just pass it all on to "junior." MTS™ can find you stocks that can turn ten thousand into 200k or more within 3 to five years.

MTS™ will not let you hold on to losses. It will get you out when losses are very small and reasonable. What is it with us that we must hold on to losers? There must be hard wiring that tells us we have to hold on to that old "piece of crap" in the driveway. Why hold on to it? Because we think it "might" be worth something some day. Or, we shove all our prized possessions into a rat hole on some shelf, only to wonder why we kept such worthless junk when we rediscover it ten years later. Stocks are no different. Clean your portfolio (house) of stocks when they show losses. Stocks that are losers turn into those *"might be worth something"* possessions that have, in reality, become worthless. Keep what works! Keep what's making you money.

Do you rely on tips or rumors of split announcements and other news stories? Do you listen to "guru" advisory recommendations or opinions from supposed market experts on television? Where do you get your information? Is it proven? Is there any kind of track record or back test tool? Do you know anything about the so-called guru's risk controls or calculators? Do you get haphazard random picks from just *anyone*? MTS™ is

a fixed process. You know exactly what you're getting and why. You can test historical signals then measure and calculate risk on every transaction.

Messing with Fundamentals

Do fundamentals matter? Does knowing anything about current fundamentals really give you any valuable trade information? News is the most *irrelevant* "fundamental" tool you could use in trading. I don't consider it fundamental simply because I don't need it. News will never make you money. Remember, "Buy on the rumor; sell on the news?" MTS™ will get you into stocks as they start the trend while the news reports rumors, not *facts*. Fundamental facts may not actually show up in the news until months later, at which point, it is usually time to sell. Stocks are forward-looking. Current price can include expectations as far out as six to 12 months.

Do you get sick of looking for stocks? Or, are you only comfortable buying stocks you are familiar with? You may feel comfortable buying stock in Costco, Microsoft, Intel, Google, or IBM because you're familiar with them. There is nothing wrong with buying these stocks if they trade well and provide high reward to risk. If you're sticking with buying stocks you feel comfortable with or those that are popular, you're missing out on the genuine big winners by playing it safe with only the stocks you know. MTS™ will find you hundreds of stocks that are trending...stocks that have high reward to risk ratios and that are ready to move today, with only a few clicks. By the time you're done with this book, you will have this fear out of your system. This course is going to show you what you've been missing.

Cashing In Small "Easy-to-Take" Profits While Keeping the Losers

I spend a lot of time on this topic in chapters 4 and 5. In a nutshell, you want to keep the stocks that are working for you...not the ones that are losing you money.

Worrying Too Much about Taxes and Commissions

If you don't want to sell because you're worried about taxes and commissions, then by all means hold on until your winner becomes a loser and don't pay any taxes at all.

Speculating Too Heavily in Options or Futures

Some investors speculate too heavily on options or futures because they believe that doing so will get them rich quickly. You've probably heard, "FX is hot...so hot that you can make a sick amount of money in a very short amount of time." This is probably another tag line you've heard. You've gone to the seminar, read the book and got the T-shirt. Then, on your first heavily-leveraged Forex trade you get blasted out of the water before you could even say, "Wire transfer." Speculation has its place, but that place is not in your core methods.

Decisions Require You to Make Up Your Mind

A decision needs to be made. So, why can't you make up your mind? Too often, the reason is because you have no business making trades in the first place when you're not prepared. Why just throw your money to the wind? Trading is not gambling, no matter what some people say. Those who believe that stock trading is like gambling would be better off going to the gaming tables and enjoying a drink.

And the biggest mistake of all is not listening to the market. In what trend is the market, currently? Is it in a Bear market, yet you try to buy stocks only to get spanked on each and every failed breakout? Missing a new Bull market is almost criminal, yet many traders are skittish at the very time they should be *dumping* buckets of money into the market. Their delay on this call to action is because too much emotion is involved in their trading decisions.

There is No Such Thing as a Paper Loss

If you think to yourself, 'I can't sell my stocks because I don't want to take a loss,' then you assume that what *you* want has some bearing on the situation. The stock doesn't know you and it most certainly doesn't care what you want. Besides, selling doesn't give you the loss. You already have the loss on your brokerage statement if you believe that you won't really lose that value until you sell. If you think to yourself, 'I haven't lost because I haven't sold,' you're just kidding yourself. That thought is **the most** asinine

idea a trader can ever have. It's like denying that you have been bitten in half by a shark because you haven't gotten out of the water yet!

Therefore, there are no *real* losses or *paper* losses: there are only losses. I'm not referring to tax implications of realized or unrealized gains or losses. I'm stating that if the value on your statement this month is less than the value it was last month, you've experienced a loss: the money is gone. The terms "paper loss" and "real loss" are irrelevant. A loss is a loss, regardless of the term's usage. Whether you have sold the stock or not doesn't matter: the money is gone.

The larger the loss, the more "real" it will become. For example, if you pay fifty dollars per share for 100 shares of XYZ and it's now worth thirty-eight dollars per share, you will have $3,800 worth of stock that would have cost you five grand. You would have experienced a $1,200 loss. Whether you decided to convert the stock to cash or hold on, the stock would have been worth only thirty-eight hundred dollars. Even though you didn't sell, you still took a loss as the stock dropped in price. You would have been better off selling and going back to cash where you would be able to think more objectively.

When you hold on to a big loser, you're rarely able to think clearly. Instead, you may falsely rationalize and say, "The stock can't go any lower." Remember, there are many other stocks from which to choose that can give you a better chance of recouping your losses. Sell the loser and move on.

Notes and Comments

Chapter 4
Decision and Trade Management

Contents

continued

TRENDS
UNIVERSITY

Contents continued

In *Chapter 2: What is Market Trend Signal™?,* we learned about the first three steps concerning market direction, using StrengthRank™ to find leading stocks and identifying stock direction. This chapter explains *Step Five: Trade Decisions* and *Step Six: Trade Management* of the MTS™ trading system.

As traders, we all want to make wise trade decisions. MTS™ gives specific signals to make your trade decisions effortless. You simply need to set up an order with your broker. We'll start out explaining several order types that you can place to ensure successful entry and exit of your trades.. Then we'll move on to specific formulas and strategies, all of which can be used together or separately to limit your losses and increase your gains using the MTS™ system.

Order Types

Before we can get into specific guidelines for proper decision and trade management, you need to have a fundamental understanding of the different kinds of orders that can be placed, since they are critical to good money management. Money management is covered in depth in *Chapter 5: Money Management.*

Market Orders

A market order is an order to buy or sell a stock or option at the best available market price. The only advantage to a market order is it will be filled quickly. Otherwise, you should not use a market order since the price at which the trade will be filled can't be guaranteed. The only time you would use a market order is if you are trying to get *out* of a losing trade that is quickly moving against you.

In the next section, we'll be talking about *limit orders*. I want to take this opportunity however, to tell you that when a losing trade is moving against you, it would be foolish to place a limit order to try to save a few decimal points. A limit order price may never be reached, leaving you stuck in the trade losing even more money.

Limit Orders

A limit order is an order to buy or sell a stock or option at a specified price or at a better price. A limit order guarantees the price at which the order is filled, provided that the limit price is reached by the stock. The only drawback to using a limit order is that the stock may never reach the price specified by the order and the trade will never be filled, causing you to miss an occasional trading opportunity. However, the advantages of using a limit order far outweigh the disadvantages.

Stop Orders

A stop order is an order to buy or sell stock at the current market price once it passes through a specified price. A stop order is generally used to close losing trades. For example, fictitious company XYZ stock is purchased at $52 per share and the exit price (the price you want to sell the stock) for a losing trade is set at forty-eight dollars. You would use a stop order, placing it to close the trade once the stock price hits the exit price of $48 per share. Once the stock hits the exit price, the order becomes a market order where your shares become available to sell at the best available market price.

Stop Limit Orders

A stop limit order works like a stop order, except that once the price trades through the specified stop price the order becomes a *limit* order. You use a stop limit order to set a specific price range for orders you want to execute, either buy or sell. The disadvantage of setting the stop limit order is that it can only get filled at that *exact* price if the stop price and limit price are the same. You do *not* want to set these at the same price!

The reason a stop limit order is used in the first place is to exit the trade should the price suddenly move against the desired direction. If this occurs and the price moves through the stop limit price and remains unfilled, your order will *not* get filled. In fact, your limit order will not get filled until the stock resumes trading at that specific price. This could cause the trade to lose even more money.

You may think this odd, but here's an example of what *not* to do. The purpose here is to show you why stop limit orders are not recommended to initiate a sell. Let's say you buy fictitious company XYZ stock at $52 and set a stop limit of forty-eight dollars—both the *stop* and the *limit* price are set to $48. The next morning, the stock gaps lower to $46. Because your order tells the broker, "I'm only willing to sell (limit price) at forty-eight dollars," and the stock drops through $48 (stop price) and is now trading at $46, your order will *not* fill because the price gapped or jumped right over the limit price straight to $46. If the stock continued to fall to $20 you would hate that order. A rule of thumb: never use stop limit orders to sell.

If you must, make sure to avoid setting the stop and limit to the *same* price. It's better, for example, to set the stop at $48 and the limit at forty-five dollars. By setting the prices apart from one another, you're telling your broker, "I am willing to sell the stock for anything less than $48 (stop price) but *no less* than $45 (limit price)." Then the sell order will trigger at the open price of $46. If the stock price hits anywhere between the stop and the limit, then your order will be filled.

Examples of using stop orders properly are covered throughout the rest of the chapter.

Order Restrictions

An order restriction is a qualifier that can be placed on any type of order, assuring that certain conditions will be met.

Good-Till-Canceled (GTC) Orders

A Good-Till-Canceled order which is otherwise known as a "GTC" remains in effect until it is filled, canceled, or until your broker's specified order time frame expires. For example, if a GTC restriction is placed on May 10 and it is not filled or canceled, it will automatically cancel on June 30. This time frame can vary for some brokers. GTCs can be used to both enter and exit trades.

Day Orders

A day order is a *limit* order that is good only for the trading day on which it is placed. If the order is not filled by the end of the trading day, it will automatically be canceled. If you want to place the order again, it must be placed the following trading day.

Formulas and Strategies

Now that we have discussed the various types of orders and order restrictions, let's look at several ways that you can use simple formulas and strategies to enhance your trading expertise.

Determining Stop Loss Pricing

A stop loss is a predetermined price at which a losing trade will be closed. A stop loss can be thought of as a mental strategy where you are mentally aware that it is time to exit a losing trade once it hits a certain price. It can also be considered a physical strategy where a stop loss order can be placed after the trade is entered and sits on your broker's books until the stop order is either triggered or canceled.

The strategy of using a predetermined price to exit a losing trade is fundamental. Setting a minimum value of a stock and giving this information to your broker in advance will certainly mitigate your trade losses. Therefore, using a stop loss is essential to effective trading practices.

The Money Stop Formula

A money stop is based on a predetermined amount of money that you are willing to lose on each trade. For example, if the most you are willing to lose on a trade is $200, then you'll need to figure out the price required to get out of a losing trade. A simple way to do your calculation is to use a money stop formula. Divide the money stop amount by the number of shares. The examples below give us two uses for the formula.

Example A
$200 ÷ 100 shares = 2 points (2 dollars)

Example B
$200 ÷ 500 shares = $0.40 cents

Table 4.1. Calculation examples to determine a price to get out of a losing trade using the money stop formula.

In Table 4.1 example A, divide $200 (the money stop amount) by 100, which is the number of shares at risk. The result is "2 points." This means that if the stock price drops by two dollars (2 points), you will have lost what you were willing to risk, e.g. all $200. At that point, your stop order that you set two dollars *lower* than your buy price would trigger which will allow you to exit the trade without suffering an unacceptable loss. The money stop calculation gives you a target price to risk on your investment.

Example B uses the same money stop amount of $200, but increases the number of risked shares to five hundred. With more shares on the line, you have a much bigger trade position. As a result, a smaller price movement in the stock would cause you to reach your risk level with only a forty cent drop.

The Percent Stop Formula

A percent stop is set by deciding the *percentage* of the trade you are willing to lose. For example, if 100 shares of XYZ stock are purchased at fifty dollars, the total investment would be $5,000. If five percent is the risked amount, then you would exit the trade after losing two hundred fifty dollars. To calculate the exit price, divide the risk amount by the number of shares. The resulting number is the number of points the stock can move until the exit price is triggered. Simply subtract the number of points (dollars) from the purchase price.

Example C
$250 ÷ 100 shares = 2.50 points, $50 - 2.50 = $47.50

Table 4.2. Calculation examples to determine a percentage of risk to get out of a losing trade using the percent stop formula.

In Table 4.2 example C, you're using the total investment amount of five thousand dollars (not shown in the equation). You want to risk only 5% of your total investment, so you'll do a quick calculation to resolve the percent stop amount (e.g., $5,000 X .05 = $250). Therefore, the first value in the equation is the percent stop amount, which is $250—the amount of money you're willing to risk on this trade.

In the example, you have 100 shares at risk, originally purchased at $50 dollars per share. Your objective is to determine the lowest share price that the stock could fall to so that you can stay within your acceptable level of risk to your capital. Remember that the amount you are willing to risk is $250. To calculate, divide the percent stop amount by 100 (e.g., $250 / 100). The product is $2.50 or 2.5 points.

Now that you know that the stock can drop $2.50 before reaching your risk limit, you finish up by calculating the price you should set *for the stop order*. The original value of the stock is fifty dollars per share. Simply subtract $2.50 from the original stock value to figure a price to exit the trade (e.g., $50 - $2.50), which gives you a stop order value of $47.50—the price at which you will sell the shares.

The Time Stop Strategy

A time stop keeps the trade open for a certain amount of time, after which the trade is closed. For example, you could sell after 30 or sixty days if the stock has not performed as expected. Time stops help manage trades that really aren't going anywhere, enabling the trader to free up funds for other trading opportunities. A time stop is usually used in conjunction with other types of stops. Setting appropriate stop loss points will be discussed in further detail in an upcoming chapter.

Avoiding Typical Emotional Cycles of Buying and Selling

You may have seen a chart like the one in Figure 4.1 which shows a common emotional pattern that traders experience—typical side effects of stock trading. The chart displays the relationship between a trader's feelings of optimism to a condition when a stock's value rises. Clearly, the chart displays the trader's anticipation of increased profits, the thrill of big gains, and the euphoria of big time gains. So now what? In the midst of all the excitement, many traders face hard decisions. It's at the time of highest vulnerability that many begin to think, 'should I sell now or should I just hold on to see if this baby is going to double again?'

What have you done in the past? Maybe you decided to Hold, having no clear exit strategy. At first, you begin to feel the anxiety of a pull back, then you experience denial, telling yourself, "It's just a minor pull back...this thing is getting ready to sail to new highs!"

Next, when you realize your optimism isn't paying off, fear sets in. It is a fear that this trend is over and you should have sold it a long time ago. You feel desperate, now that all of your gains are being wiped out. The mounting emotion may lead to panic. You may very well be underwater and losing your principal capital. After panic, capitulation arrives. You ask yourself, "How could I have been so wrong?" or, "Why didn't I sell when I had such a nice gain?"

Finally you bail out, sell the stock, become increasingly despondent, and sink into a depression. This scenario is a roller-coaster ride you do not need.

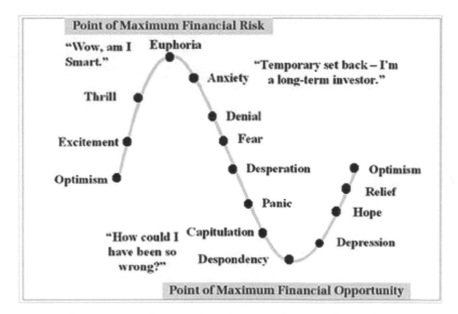

Figure 4.1. Chart displaying emotional patterns common to stock traders. (Original source unknown.)

You may tell yourself you're a pathetic trader and a worthless excuse for a human being. You may believe that you will never trade stocks again. You also may decide to "analyze" your process to see what went wrong, realize your mistakes, but don't do anything about them. Instead, you patch yourself up and go along for another ride, never learning how to fix your mistakes and never making progress.

Let's go through several specific examples of exactly what you would be looking for and how to enter and exit a trade using the MTS™ system.

The Bear market of 2008 and '09 was quick and brutal. Prices plummeted to near catastrophic lows. Many stocks had been beaten into bankruptcy. Many investment firms and banks were bailed out by government interventions while investors who weren't offered aid were smacked down to generational lows.

On March 12th The Market Trend Newsletter noted:

> The Market Trend Signal™ is a mild Bear/Bear market. Based on the close, the signal calculation is literally .009 from being mild Bull, so unless we open tomorrow below the low (won't happen), this signal will turn to mild Bull. Conditions are much improved to buy stocks. Traders should trade with a Bullish bias. Investors should buy high-ranking, Buy rated stocks. Screen for high-ranking (over 90) stocks that have moved to BUY from HOLD and/or that had ST trend movement from DN (down) to UP. This will provide stocks that are ready to move or continue their current moves.

On that same day, Apple Inc (AAPL) was showing a HOLD ST trend UP. Conditions were improving to buy high-ranking stocks.

On March 17th, The Market Trend Newsletter stated:

> The Market Trend Signal™ conditions are a mild Bull/Bear market. Traders should trade with a Bullish bias. Investors should buy high-ranking, Buy rated stocks or Bullish ETFs.

AAPL changed ratings, going from HOLD to BUY. Conditions were ideal for the stock market and all strong stocks to perform very well.

TRENDS
UNIVERSITY

Figure 4.2. Apple Inc (AAPL) candlestick chart showing promising ratings changes, going from HOLD to BUY.

You would have logged into the site on the 17th day of March and at the close of the market, you would have had a very clear BUY rating on the stock. This was where the next steps should have taken place—you should have bought stock. To buy, you would have entered an order to buy at the open of the next trading day with a simple transaction method called an "EOD" or "end of day" trading method.

Before we go on, I want you to notice two things in Figure 4.2. First, notice all the green Buy ratings on the chart about a month prior the March 17 signal. Those are legitimate signals and are all trades that would have been taken. Because the MTS™ had a MILD BULL condition and the stock had a BUY signal, we should make the trade. The only possible indicator that the trade might fail is that the MTS™ also indicated a Bear market versus a Bull market.

Using the trend following, you will find that trend tops and bottoms may create whipsaws or false signals. These false signals are the price we pay as traders to catch the real trend when it develops.

TRENDS UNIVERSITY

Buying the first Buy signal on February 17 would have produced a stopped-out trade on the next Sell signal which came on March 9. A loss of just over thirteen percent would have resulted on the trade. If you had ten percent of your account in the trade, it would have produced a 1.3% drawdown of your trading balance, which would have been an insignificant loss.

The second point I want to make is that the signal was not given at the 82-84 range. It was given at the 95-100 range (*see* Figure 4.2). This matters because it is very important at this stage to be perfectly clear in your mind that you will *never* pick the *exact* top or bottom. If you believe that you need to get in at the exact bottom and get out at the exact top, you will probably not succeed in trading and you may as well go bet on the horses or go to Vegas. Trying to pick tops and bottoms is nothing more than trying to cast wagers. The odds are grossly not in your favor.

Not picking the bottom doesn't mean you can't get pretty darn close. The MTS™ ST Trend Signal™ is designed to get you into an early trend at the earliest possible confirmation point. In Figure 4.3, ST Trend signals are an early indication of a new trend shift.

Figure 4.3. ST Trend signals are an early indication of a new trend shift.

Now, let's return to the trade example. It's the evening after the market has closed and you have reviewed the scans and found the trade, or you have reviewed your watch list and found that your favorite stock now has a Buy rating. Now is the time to go through the mechanics of setting up the transaction in your brokerage account. Entering trades using the MTS™ system should always be done at the open following the BUY signal (*see* Figure 4.4).

Figure 4.4. Entering trades using the MTS™ system should always be done at the open following the BUY signal.

Most, if not all brokerage accounts allow you to set up an order before the market opens or after it closes. This is not "after hours" trading. This is simply being able to set up an order contingent upon certain events.

Figure 4.5. A common look to most broker order forms. Order form of www.tdameritrade.com

The best kind of order to make is a buy stop limit order. This means you will select the number of shares you want to buy and set a limit price. The *limit* price is the price at which you are willing to buy the stock—or better. The *stop* price is the price you're not willing to pay *any less than* to get in on the trade.

Taking a closer look at this example, let's say that at the end of the day, the closing price on AAPL is $99.66. You look at the stock and make a risk management decision. You ask yourself a couple of questions: "What if the stock gaps higher in the morning, e.g. the stock opens much higher than the previous day's closing price?" and, "What price am I still willing to pay?"

In this example, if you're not willing to pay any more than one hundred five dollars and are willing to pay any amount less than that all the way to your *stop price* of $90, then you would submit a buy stop limit order with the *limit* price of $105 and a *stop* price of ninety. Once you have submitted the order—that evening or the next morning before the market opens—your order will trigger immediately upon the market open, as long as the price opens *within your range*.

You may or may not get the exact open price, but it will usually be close. If the stock gapped up to $110 at the open, your order would *not* fill because it is greater than the one hundred five dollar *limit* price (top). If it gapped down to $89, again, your order would not be filled because the price was lower than your *stop* price of ninety.

In Figures 4.6 and 4.7, we can see that as of October 26, 2009 the trade we are using as our example is up 102%! This is trading stocks at its best. We are not day traders. We want to stay in a trade as long as it stays a BUY or a HOLD, which can last months.

Date	Signal	Price	Trade Profit/Loss	$10000
2/17/2009	Buy	$96.87		$10000
3/9/2009	Sell	$84.18	▼ 13.10 %	$8690
3/18/2009	Buy	$99.91		$8690
10/26/2009	Current	$202.48	▲ 102.66 %	$17611

Figure 4.6. Apple Inc (AAPL) trade signal history using MTS™ back test for 2009.

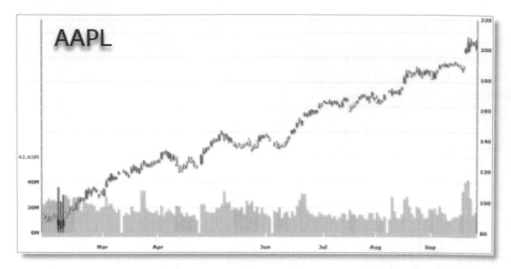

Figure 4.7. Apple Inc (AAPL) performance chart displaying close-of-day 26 Oct 2009's phenomenal trade profit.

When to Successfully Get Out of Losers and Exit Winners

In this section, we're going to discuss two of the most important aspects of trade management. The first aspect is when to get out of your winners. The second aspect is when to get out of your losers. What's your current approach to getting out of your winners? Do you use a price target or how about a percentage target? Has that been working for you?

Have you experienced the wonderful feeling of taking profits then the very next day the stock rallies 10%, then another five—never giving you a pull back—only to move up another fifty or even 80%? Do you just blow it off by saying, "Well, at least I made *some* money on it?" My guess is that these words sound familiar. I think every trader has experienced this disappointment. Trend following is a different game than many other traders play. Our goal is to maximize on our winners for as long as possible. We have the tools to buy more at points where others would exit prematurely and take maximum gains while others take limited profits.

80

How and Why to Enter and Exit the Market

Look at another example of how to enter a trade. In this example, we'll focus on a stock that has had its rating changed from HOLD to BUY in the last day. These criteria can be entered into the Stock Screener and a list of resulting stocks with these criteria will be displayed.

You can filter search results by StrengthRank™ and pick the highest one on the list as a selection. The buy should be made the morning after the Buy signal is given, as you can see in Figures 4.8 and 4.9. The best order to place is a buy stop limit order. You will also attach your stop loss order to the buy order so that once the buy order is filled it will set up your stop loss automatically. Most brokerages allow you to set up these triggered orders.

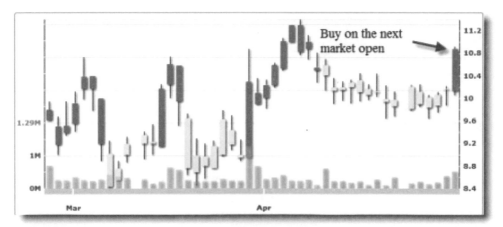

Figure 4.8. Candlestick chart showing examples of EOD (end of day) signals.

Figure 4.9. Buying on the opening price the day after the BUY signal is given.

The initial placement of a stop loss is critical. The first trade is dealing with your capital when there are no gains yet to "let ride." Your capital is your baby, it is your nugget. You treat it with love and respect and you protect it like one of your children.

There is no excuse for delay or for waiting to see how it turns out. Waiting to see without a plan does not work. When you go into a trade you will know exactly what your risk is on each and every trade and what those risks will mean to your capital if or when you're wrong.

The first stop location should be the most recent low on the chart before the BUY signal is given. Take a look at our example in Figure 4.9. The BUY signal is given at $10.77 and the lowest point on the chart before the new BUY signal is nine dollars sixty cents. This amount gives us a $1.17 risk or nearly an eleven percent loss should we get stopped out of this trade.

Notice in Figure 4.10 that the stock goes through retracements in the UP trend, but ideally will not generate a SELL signal during those pull backs. If no Sell signal is given, then the stop can be adjusted higher to the new low of the retracement. The stop adjustment dates are the first Buy signal after a HOLD signal in the UP trend. The plan is to hold onto the trade until you get a new Sell signal.

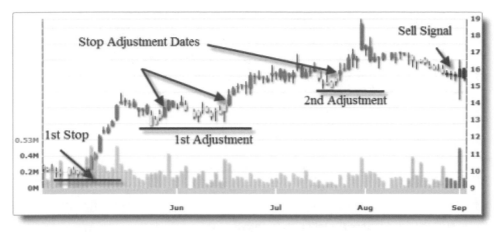

Figure 4.10. Stops are adjusted higher on the first BUY signal after a HOLD signal.

The stop adjustment process for winners is the same as the plan described in the past few pages, but let me just summarize. Using Figure 4.10, we can see that after a BUY signal is given and you buy the stock, your initial stop gets placed below the lowest price before the BUY signal is given.

You "trail" or adjust your stop loss higher after the stock has retraced to a HOLD rating then moved back to a BUY rating (*see* Figure 4.10). Place your stop below the *lowest* low before the new Buy rating is given, all within the same upward trend. You now have a fixed date and process to know exactly when and how to adjust your stops with winning trades. This ensures that you lock in a profit after the first adjustment.

TRENDS
UNIVERSITY

Figure 4.11. First SELL signal since the initial trade entry.

Be alert to the idea that you may get stopped out, when the stock may not be finished with the UP trend. If you get stopped out and a Sell signal has not yet been given, enter the trade on the next Buy signal.

Adjusting Stops when Trades are Losers

Never, and I repeat, *never* move your stop *lower*. If you are given a Sell signal or are stopped out of a trade, the trade is over. Take your losses and either move on to a new stock or simply wait for the next Buy signal for that same stock. It does not matter that you might buy it again at a price higher than it was sold. Consider it a whole new trade with different parameters.

The MTS™ Buying Process

Use these simple steps to ensure a better buying strategy.

1. Locate the new BUY signal on a stock in the MTS™ system,
2. Set up a buy stop limit order with your broker,

TRENDS
UNIVERSITY

3. Set up a contingent stop loss order and attach it to the Buy order so it is set up once the Buy signal is triggered,
4. Place Stop loss under the swing low or countertrend low before the Buy signal (the first stop location is the recent low),
5. Monitor trades once a day in your watch list to determine if a stop adjustment is necessary,
6. Adjust stop loss higher after the stock has gone from HOLD back to BUY,
7. Add to position if desired on the open the day after the signal has gone from HOLD back to BUY, and
8. Sell on the opening morning after the SELL signal is given. Enter a sell stop limit order with your broker or sell if your stop is triggered, whichever comes first.

When to Get Out of a Losing Position

In this example, you have a stock that is showing a loss, meaning you bought the stock and it immediately went down and is now trading at a price less than your purchase price. So, when do you cut your losses? The key is to have a plan. You must know exactly what you're going to do to take care of your losers as well as your winners.

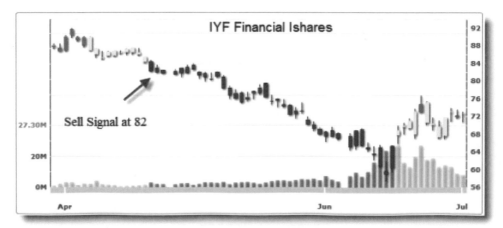

Figure 4.12. SELL signal for iShares Dow Jones US Financial Sector (IYF).

Let's talk about two ways to know exactly how to get out of losers. In trading, you need to get very familiar with the phrase, "Your first loss is your best loss." The first method in the MTS™ system is to use the SELL signal as your exit signal. In Figure 4.12, we can see the way this looks on the chart. Simply watch the stock you own in the MTS™ watch list. When the system posts a SELL, enter a Sell order for the next morning and exit the trade at the market open. The second method of selling is your stop loss.

On May 21, 2008 the iShares Dow Jones US Financial Sector (IYF) was given a SELL signal in the MTS™ system. If you owned this ETF, you would enter a Sell order at one of two times: 1) the evening the signal was received, or 2) the morning after the signal—before the market opens. Entering a Sell order at either of these times will get you out of the trade at the market open.

Margin: Investing with Borrowed Money

Did you know that if you have at least a few thousand dollars in your brokerage account that you might qualify to borrow money against your existing stocks to buy even more? This practice is known as "trading on margin," and it allows you to get very aggressive to buy more shares of a company than you could otherwise afford.

Essentially defined, the term "margin" means "investing with borrowed money." You may purchase stock on margin by borrowing money (once you're qualified) from your broker at a 9.5% fixed interest rate, for example. The interest rate is determined by each brokerage firm and normally decreases as the amount borrowed increases (e.g., an investor borrowing $500,000 will pay a substantially lower rate than one borrowing five thousand).

Margin Maintenance Requirements

Each brokerage firm establishes a margin maintenance requirement. This maintenance requirement is the percentage equity the investor must keep in his portfolio at all times. A broker that maintains a thirty percent maintenance requirement, for example, would lend up to $2.33 for every dollar an investor has deposited in his account, giving the investor $3.33 of assets with which to invest. An investor with a small balance in his portfolio may be subject to a higher maintenance requirement (typically 50%) because the broker believes the risk associated with this kind of account is greater.

The Power of Leverage: Practical Examples of Margin in Action

Now that we know the basics of margin and broker maintenance requirements, we're going to create a practical example of how to use margin as trading leverage.

Let's say that you deposit $10,020 into your margin-approved brokerage account. The firm has a generic fifty percent maintenance requirement and is currently charging 8% interest on loans valued less than fifty thousand dollars. In this example, you decide to purchase stock in a company. Normally, you would be limited to the $10,020 cash you have at your disposal. Utilizing margin, however, you borrow just under the maximum amount allowable—ten thousand dollars in this case, giving you a grand total of $20,020 to invest. You pay a twenty dollar brokerage commission and use the $20,000; half of which is your own money, the other half is money borrowed from your broker to buy 1,332 shares of the company at fifteen dollars each.

Long Scenario 1

The stock falls to ten dollars per share. The portfolio now has a market value of $13,320 (e.g., $10 per share x $1,332 shares). Since ten thousand of that is cash from the margin loan, $3,320, or twenty-five percent of the margin loan is your equity. Why does this pose a serious problem? You must restore your equity to 50% within twenty-four hours or you broker will liquidate your position to pay the outstanding balance on the margin loan. This 24 hour notice is known as a "margin call." To meet your margin call in this scenario, you will have to deposit cash or shares of stock worth at least $6,680.

Had you not bought *on margin*, your loss would have been limited to $3,333. You would have also had the freedom to ignore the fall in market value if you believed the company was a bargain. Your use of margin, however, has turned your loss into -$6,680 plus the commission on the forced sale of stock and the interest expense on the outstanding balance.

Long Scenario 2

After purchasing 1,332 shares of stock at fifteen dollars apiece, the price rises to $20. Thus, the market value of the portfolio is now $26,640. You sell the stock, pay back the ten thousand dollar margin loan and pocket $6,640 before paying the interest and selling commission. Had you *not* utilized margin, this transaction would have only earned you a profit of $3,333 before commissions.

The lesson that you need to take away is that margin amplifies a portfolio's performance; it makes losses and gains greater than they would have been if the trade had been on a strict cash-only basis. The primary risks are market and time. Prices may fall or a significant amount of time may be needed for the price of a stock to rise, resulting in higher interest costs to you. Margin adds an additional level of risk, but when conditions are right, such as buying when MTS™ is Bullish in a Bull market, it can blow the roof off your account.

The best way to get started with margin is to only use a small amount that is available to you. For example, you have $10,000 in your account. With margin, you have ten thousand dollars of additional funds available to you. The first rule: *don't* use all funds that may be available to you. Instead, start out borrowing no more than $2,000 for this example or 20% percent of your account until you are comfortable with how it works.

Trading Bearish Strategies

The Art of Shorting Stocks

Let's say I own one hundred shares of fictitious company XYZ at $50 per share. You, being my trading associate, believe that the stock price will crash sometime soon. You are so convinced that the stock will crash that you come to me and ask to borrow my hundred shares of XYZ and sell them at the current market price of $50. I agree to lend you my shares as long as you pay me back a hundred shares of the same stock at some arbitrary point in the future. You take the hundred borrowed shares, sell them for $5,000 and pocket the money (e.g., 100 shares x $50 per share = $5,000).

The following week, the price of XYZ stock falls to $20 per share. You call your broker and tell him to buy one hundred shares of the stock at the new, lower price. You pay your broker two thousand dollars (e.g., 100 shares x $20 per share = $2,000). A few days later, you pick up the shares of XYZ and bring them by my office. "Here are the hundred shares I borrowed," you say, as you put them on my desk.

Did you follow what just happened? You borrowed *my* shares of XYZ and sold them for five grand. The following week, when XYZ fell to $20 per share, you *repurchased* those

hundred shares for $2,000 and gave them back to me. In the meantime, you pocketed the difference of $3,000. This is what we refer to as "shorting stock."

The Speculative Nature of Shorting Stock

What if the price of XYZ stock had risen? The person shorting stock would have had to buy back the shares at the new, higher price and absorb the loss, personally. Unlike being long the stock where your losses are limited to the amount of capital you invest (e.g., if you invest $100, you cannot lose more than your one hundred dollar investment), shorting stock has *no limit* to the amount you might ultimately lose. In the unlikely event that the stock had shot up to $1,000, you would have had to purchase a hundred shares at one thousand dollars per share for a total investment of $100,000. Taking into account the five thousand dollar proceeds you gained from selling the shares earlier, you would have *lost* $95,000 on the transaction. You just lost your house, pal. Understand the risk here? Theoretically, this could happen. In reality, the odds of it happening are very slim.

Some investors practice shorting stock as a hedge to protect their portfolio and to profit from a market down turn. In most cases, this is neither required nor is it recommended for most investors.

The MTS™ system works amazingly well using long only strategies—buying stocks on the Buy signals and selling them on the Sell signals. Coupling these long only strategies with the knowledge of how to short stocks will increase your edge. The critical keys to your success are: 1) knowing how to employ shorting strategies; 2) defining your risk limit; and 3) knowing how to properly manage both of them. This knowledge can juice up your returns—just remember the example of Tenneco, Inc. (TEN) in chapter 1.

In order to begin shorting stock, you must open a margin account with your brokerage firm. You will be charged interest on the borrowed funds and your activities will be subject to several rules and regulations that govern how you can short stock—for example, you cannot short a penny stock. After taking these factors into consideration, you will realize that shorting stock is not, in most cases, a financially-fattening activity.

One reason people don't like to short too often is that potential returns are just not as spectacular as what can be achieved on the upside. Even if a stock drops from fifty dollars to $.50, you can only make one hundred percent on your money. The reason why shorting does not pay off as well is because shorting requires margin and margin requires you to actually have collateral in your account. You can't just open a margin account with a zero balance then go short a thousand shares of IBM at fifty dollars and have a cool $50,000 deposited to your account. Your account, prior to engaging this size of a short trade would need to have a minimum balance of $25,000.

When you sell short, SEC Regulation T imposes an initial margin requirement of 150%. This sounds extreme, but the first hundred percent of the requirement can be satisfied by the proceeds of the short sale, leaving just 50% for you to maintain in margin. To keep a short position, maintenance requires a margin of $5 per share or thirty percent of the current market value, whichever is greater.

To see how the numbers look, let's say you short $10,000 worth of stock. You must have stock with a loan value of at least $5,000 to comply with Regulation T. Keeping things simple, you deposit cash. At the end of the sale, the credit balance consists of the ten thousand dollars in proceeds from the short sale plus the $5,000 deposit.

Long Market	Short Market	Credit Balance	Debit Balance	Equity
$ 0.00	$ 10,000.00	$ 15,000.00	$ 0.00	$ 5,000.0

Table 4.3. Example of short sale cash requirement.

Short Selling Best Practices: The Value of Using Buy/Sell Stop Limit Orders

Let's look at a "best practices" short example. On September 18, 2008, you deposit $10,000 into your trading account. You have been following Aeropostale Inc (ARO) in your watch list and see that it just posted a new SELL rating the same day. You log in to your brokerage account and set up a contingent order to short the stock at the open tomorrow morning. You set up a *sell stop limit* order, knowing that the *stop* price is the swing high (recent counter trend high see Figure 4.13) before the SELL signal. You also set the *limit* price—a price you are not willing to pay less than to establish your short position.

To illustrate the value of using a sell stop limit order, let's add this possibility to the scenario. Your trade parameters are: *sell stop limit* price is $37.22 with a *limit* price set to $32. The purpose of creating a sell stop limit is to ensure that you don't short (sell to open) a stock that is less than your limit price.

Let's create a case-in-point where the unthinkable happens—a scenario requiring a sell stop limit order. The night before you set up the trade, ARO comes out with news that all teenagers the world over are boycotting clothes. Since Aeropostale is *"the* bomb" teen clothing line which has suddenly been boycotted, the stock will open significantly lower than the previous day's close—meaning that the stock will gap down.

According to pre-market trading indications, the new open price is $15 per share. You do not want your order to sell short the ARO stock now because this is such a large drop you need to reconsider your risk criteria. Because you used a *limit* price of $32 your order will not be placed at the opening price of $15 because it is lower than your limit price. Remember that by placing the *limit* order, you're telling your broker you don't want to short (sell to open) at any price less than $32.

Now you can reevaluate your strategy for ARO because you're not in an unwanted trade. It's important to note that if you had used a sell stop order and had *not* set a limit price, you would have ended up entering that trade. It's easy to see that stop limit orders give you better control over your transactions.

In reality, the ARO stock did not gap down and the scenario didn't play out that way at all. Our purpose was to give you knowledge about what could happen to your order if you had not used a limit price. The limit price in an opening stop limit order—in this case, sell to open—is critical to giving you full control of your order. If the stock did drop to $15, then we would welcome it "after" we had already established our short trade.

Let's go back to the start and continue with the order setup. Recall that it is September 18, 2008, and you deposit $10,000 into your trading account. You have been following Aeropostale (ARO) in your watch list and see that it just posted a new SELL rating the same day. You log in to your brokerage account and set up a contingent order to short the stock at the open tomorrow morning.

This time, you remember to set a sell stop limit order with your broker, telling him that you are willing to sell short ARO at any price *no more* than $37.22 (the *stop* price) and *no less* than $32.00, which is the *limit* price. You determine to short using your *full* margin capabilities and place the order using $20,000 of margin. We're taking advantage of the full margin in this example to show you potential returns.

Remember that Regulation T imposes an initial margin requirement of 150% on short sales—the first 100% of the margin requirement can be satisfied by the proceeds of the short sale, leaving just 50% for you to maintain in cash or stock. You put the order to sell short 550 shares using a sell (to open) stop limit order. You also attach a stop loss order for $37.22 which is the swing high before the Sell signal is given.

Let's say you've entered the trade and the stock price moves above $37.22. The trade will get stopped out, and you'll be forced to buy back the shares for a higher price than you sold them. Your stop loss order will trigger automatically in your brokerage account, resulting in a losing trade. The loss would be $1,919.52 or nearly ten and a half percent on the trade which is 19% of your cash. In this scenario, you started with ten thousand dollars of your own money. Doing some quick math, you would be left with $8,179 after you got stopped out.

Figure 4.13. Aeropostale Inc (ARO) chart showing short sale in August, then buying back to cover the short on the day after the BUY signal is given.

The next morning, ARO opens at $33.69 (*see* Figure 4.13). Let's presume that your order is triggered at that price. The sell (remember we are shorting) stop is met because the price is less than $37.22, and the limit is met because the price is greater than $32.00. Your order would immediately be triggered at the market price. You now hold $18,529 (e.g., 550 X $33.69) of proceeds from selling short the stock. This amount added to your ten thousand dollars in cash sums up to a balance of $28,529. We won't fiddle with commission numbers, as they are irrelevant for our purpose in this example.

The stock drops as you expect. You sell short the stock as it begins dropping in price. To profit when shorting, you sell high as the price of the stock begins its trend downward, trail the stop loss by moving the stop down and buy back low as the stock begins an upward trend. Note that in the case of shorting, you trail your stop *downward*, whereas in the case of long trades, you trail the stop *upward*.

Adjusting the Stop Loss on a Short Trade

In Figure 4.14, the rating for ARO has gone from SELL to HOLD. Then, the rating moves back to SELL. Now is the time to adjust the stop loss lower. As we said, the best time to

94

adjust the stop loss for a short trade is on the day the rating goes back to SELL. If the stock goes from HOLD to BUY, you would exit the trade. By buying back to cover the stock, you effectively close the short position. Once the stock bottoms, then signals HOLD then BUY, you exit the trade (buy to cover) on the open of the next morning.

Figure 4.14. Stops are moved once a HOLD signal is given followed by a SELL signal.

In Figure 4.14, the opening price is $17.90. You buy back five hundred fifty shares, spending $9,845 in the process. This transaction leaves you with an $8,662 gain or an eighty-six percent profit on your $10,000. The stock only dropped 46%, but because you used *all* your margin leverage, you made twice as much.

The MTS™ Shorting Process

Use these simple steps to ensure you are following the MTS™ system when shorting stocks. The process will assist you in finding, implementing and managing your short trades.

1. Locate a new SELL signal on a stock in the MTS™ system,

2. Set up a sell stop limit order with your broker to open (sell to open),
3. Set up a contingent stop loss order and attach it to the Sell (to open) order so it is set up once the Sell (short) is triggered,
4. Set the initial stop loss at the swing high or countertrend high before the Sell signal (the first stop location is the recent high),
5. Monitor trades once a day in your watch list to determine if a stop adjustment is necessary,
6. Adjust stop loss lower after the stock has gone from HOLD then back to SELL,
7. Add to position if desired on the open the day after the signal has gone from HOLD back to SELL, and
8. Buy (to cover) on the opening morning after the Buy signal is given. Enter a buy stop limit (to cover) order with your broker or buy (to cover) if your stop is triggered, whichever comes first.

U TRENDS
UNIVERSITY

Notes and Comments

Notes and Comments

Notes and Comments

Chapter 5
Money Management

Contents

Money management is the single most important aspect of trading. The methodology is secondary. This isn't meant to discredit the importance of having a successful method for finding trading opportunities. Rather, it means that without proper money management, even the most successful methodology can lose money. In addition, proper money management can eliminate much of the stress that accompanies trading.

Choosing a Market and Determining Entry/Exit Timing

With the advent of the Exchange Traded Funds (ETF), choosing a market and determining your best time to buy and sell is easier than ever. There exists literally hundreds of ETFs that track Indexes, Sectors, commodities, currencies, and many varieties of markets.

The MTS™ system works best when you treat a stock like its own market. The core idea behind trend following stocks is to tap into stocks' potential and trade them as if they are their own "market." Most modern portfolio theorists prefer that you diversify your

investment capital into a combination of separate, distinct markets such as stocks, bonds, cash, metals, and currencies because doing so will mitigate your investment risk. You're essentially throwing money at a little of everything in the hope that something works. If one market is not doing well, supposedly some of the other markets or "asset classes" will remain steady enough to balance out potential losses to your portfolio.

I want you to alter your thinking a bit. The concept that I want you to understand is that with the MTS™ system, there is no need to trade separate markets to mitigate your risk. The idea that you must diversity into separate "entities," "markets," or "asset classes" in order to be considered a serious, sophisticated trader simply isn't true. MTS™ incorporates StrengthRank™ to search for highly qualified stocks, giving you the ability to trade stocks for diversification just as you would with traditional markets. Being diversified entirely among stocks is still considered being diversified.

MTS™ StrengthRank™ offers you a different approach to diversification that is based on trading stocks, so you don't have to diversify into separate markets. "Traditional" diversification methods are simply for those who think everything is risky. You should diversify among stocks. When you trade high StrengthRank™ stocks, you will always be in an "asset class" with a high probability of success. This also allows you to trade in almost any kind of brokerage account, whereas you may not qualify for, or even want to open some forms of Forex or futures accounts.

Now that you understand the idea of trading each stock like its own asset class or market, how do you know *how much* to invest? There are several approaches that will help you with your decision. Our purpose in the next section is to give you a clear understanding for how to determine which of the various money management methods to use inside the MTS™ system.

The Fixed Fractional Approach

The first method in money management is called "fixed fractional" money management. It is a method that will ensure you make bigger bets when you're winning and smaller bets when you're losing. If I take bigger risks as my portfolio is having a drawdown using the "double down" idea—using logic such as, 'surely this is the *lowest* low and my account can't go much lower, so I'm going to pile into this thing and let it ride or double down,' then I will end up letting my account ride right into the dirt! Traders want to use the same approach with money management that they do with the stocks themselves. Follow the trend and trust your winners...not your losers.

Using a fixed fractional approach, you first determine how much you will allocate to each trade. You must determine both how much total capital you will commit as well as how much you're willing to lose if you get stopped out and the trade doesn't work for you. When I refer to how much should be risked on each trade, I'm referring to the percentage of the total account that would be lost if the trade ends up a loser as opposed to the total amount of equity that will be committed to the trade.

So how do you figure out how much capital you're willing to commit and how much you're willing to lose? There are many different ideas on the maximum allowable risk per trade. Some believe that no more than 3% would be best, some may say that two percent is enough, while others believe the risk should be up to 20%.

There are also many who may be starting out with only $5,000 with which to trade. Applying the fixed fractional approach using 10% at risk would require that you do not risk more than $500 in an effort to make fifteen hundred. With accounts under $5,000, risking ten percent per trade limits gains. Commission costs typically eat up a significant portion of the gain on any trade with accounts under five thousand dollars, making it very hard to grow your account unless you commit larger amounts to each trade.

Capturing Full System Potential Using Small Risk Capital

Many will find other approaches more appealing. Some traders may need to take on more risk due to smaller capital amounts they have available. For example, a trader may need to consider risking between ten and twenty percent of his trading capital on each trade if the investment amount is $10,000 or less. Keep in mind that in order to get the return, you have to take the risk. The S&P 500 averages returns around ten percent per year. It's a worthy goal to maintain and many traders believe that if they put a little bit of money into everything they will reduce their risk of losses while trying to achieve it.

It is possible to diversify away *all* of your returns. Let's say you have a $100,000 trading account and own fifty stocks—meaning that you have $2,000 in each position. If five of those stocks increase one hundred percent, the overall gain to your portfolio is 10%. While ten percent is not a bad return, there are other stocks in your portfolio that have not performed as well or may have even lost fifty percent or more of their value. Then there will be stocks that are somewhere in between. When you see ups and downs in your portfolio, you're really looking at "market-like" returns.

By diversifying into many stocks you *may* reduce your risk of loss, but you may also decrease your potential return in the process. Ultimately, if you diversify away all your returns into many stocks, you limit your gains. If this is the case, you may as well trade one broadly-diversified ETF with your entire account and save yourself the time of looking for stocks to trade. By focusing on a smaller group of stocks and putting larger percentages of your portfolio into them you will increase your odds of much larger returns. The risk can be reduced by focusing on high StrengthRank™ stocks whose ratings have gone from HOLD to BUY and have high trade expectancy. By using stocks found in the MTS™ system you find strong stocks that are big movers.

Market Trend Signal™ Money Management

The Muscle 5 and Muscle 10 Money Management Methods

One preferred way to take on the system and capture its full potential is to trade five stocks *only* and reinvest 100% of any gains back into the stock you are trading or replacing. This is called the "Muscle 5" money management method.

For example, let's say you decide to trade BONT, TEN, F, MSFT and GOOG. Look at the historical reward to risk and trade expectancy on each of these five stocks to decide whether they will provide adequate potential with minimal risk. You should look for stocks with at least a three to one (3:1) reward to risk ratio and an annualized trade expectancy of twenty percent. If they've passed the test, you should buy these stocks on each Buy signal and sell them on each Sell signal, repeating this cycle until you decide to replace one of the stocks. You may decide to replace a stock for a variety of reasons, including (but not limited to) rating changes, a change in StrengthRank™ lower, or

U TRENDS
UNIVERSITY

because you decide to shift to a stock that has produced a better reward to risk ratio (average gain divided by average loss).

Reinvesting Using the MTS™ System

Circumstances may arise where one stock starts to take up a large position in your portfolio. If the stock is working for you, i.e. making money, then there is no reason to leave it and diversify into other stocks. This activity is referred to as *rebalancing* which is common in most modern portfolio theories. If there is a need to rebalance, use the MTS™ system to find a new candidate. Rebalancing by selling big winners too soon is the reason why most funds and traders play it too safely and achieve mediocre returns.

There will be times when you actually want to start spending some of that hard-earned cash. When you have a Sell signal and exit a trade, determine at that point how much you are going to set aside for cash withdrawal. After you have determined the cash amount, reinvest everything else back into the stock you just sold. You will experience normal volatility and in some cases gut-wrenching drawdown (losses) with these five stocks. But as you will see in many upcoming examples, stocks traded within the system's parameters will recover or get replaced by better candidates. You must stick with it...keep going. You can rotate out to other stocks you find using the MTS™ Stock Screener and the *MuscleStocks* scanner. The best time to do this is after you've exited another stock based on a stop or a Sell signal. The *Muscle 10* method uses the same approach as *Muscle 5*, but you use ten stocks instead of five.

In Figure 5.1, Bon-Ton Stores Inc (BONT) stock value increased 1,244% in a little less than three years. This happened during one of the most treacherous markets in 80 years. In Figure 5.1, you can see that the twenty thousand dollar investment grew into over $249,934 of profits. In order to get that kind of return, the trader had to reinvest all gains back into the next Buy signal. In a $100,000 portfolio, twenty percent ($20,000) invested in BONT would represent one of the five stocks traded in a 5 stock portfolio.

Back Test	Equity Curve		StockSymbol	bont	

Trade Stats for	**BONT**		Current Signal	Buy	Please select buy/sell criteria
Number of Trades	11	Trade expectancy	$3900.08		☑ **Long**
Total Profit amount	$275,120.29	Trade expectancy%	39%		
Total Loss amount	$25,186.23	Annual Trade expectancy	$10,148.09		Buy / Sell
Total Profit or Total Loss	$249,934.06	Annual Trade expectancy%	101.48%		
Avg Profit on Winners	$39,302.90	Largest profit	$144,186.46		
Avg Loss on Losers	$6,296.56	Largest loss	$11,303.60		☐ **Short**
Total Net % gain or loss	1249.67%	Avg days in trade	71		Sell / Buy
Aver % gain on Winners	70.16%	Avg days between trades	79		
Aver % loss on Losers	15.52%				
Reward to Risk Ratio	4.52				Investment dollars: 20000
Number of Trades Per year	2.6				
Number of Winners	7				Additions on Signals
Number of Losers	4				☑ Compound original invesment
Winning Percentage	63.64				☐ Use fixed amount on new signal

Start date 01/01/2006   End date 03/24/2010   Query

Figure 5.1. Bon-Ton Stores Inc (BONT) trade statistics from 01/01/06 through 11/14/2009.

The 20/20 Muscle 5 Fixed Fractional Method

Another money management tool is the "20/20 Muscle 5 Fixed Fractional" method. It gives you the punch of some of these hot individual stocks you can trade. You commit 20% of capital to each of five trades and assume a maximum of twenty percent risk per trade. This means you set an initial 20% stop loss on each trade. As the trade moves in your favor, you adjust the stop according to the rules in chapter 4. The result ends up equating to placing 5% of your capital at risk on each trade.

20/20 Muscle 5 Fixed Fractional uses a fixed percentage approach that reduces your risk and diversifies your gains across all five stocks you're trading. Spreading your risk may increase the potential for positive results because you're spreading the opportunity among five instead of one.

Fixed Percent Account							
$ 100,000.00							20.00%
					Account Bal	Cum Return	% Cap at Risk
				Gain/Loss	$ 100,000.00		
$	20,000	31.82%	$ 26,364	$6,364.00	$ 106,364	6.36%	20.00%
$	21,273	44.42%	$ 30,722	$9,449.38	$ 115,813	15.81%	20.00%
$	23,163	37.97%	$ 31,958	$8,794.87	$ 124,608	24.61%	20.00%
$	24,922	-23.24%	$ 19,130	($5,791.79)	$ 118,816	18.82%	20.00%
$	23,763	14.50%	$ 27,209	$3,445.68	$ 122,262	22.26%	20.00%
$	24,452	-17.99%	$ 20,053	($4,398.99)	$ 117,863	17.86%	20.00%
$	23,573	-13.43%	$ 20,407	($3,165.80)	$ 114,697	14.70%	20.00%
$	22,939	140.00%	$ 55,055	$32,115.25	$ 146,813	46.81%	20.00%
$	29,363	210.00%	$ 91,024	$61,661.29	$ 208,474	108.47%	20.00%

Figure 5.2. Twenty percent (20%) of investment capital puts larger allocations into winning streaks and lower allocations into losing streaks.

The example in Figure 5.2 shows that a twenty thousand dollar investment grew into $88,470, increasing the starting balance of one hundred thousand (e.g., $20,000 X 5 = $100,000) to $208,474. Notice that on each new buy you only reinvest twenty percent of your new account balance. As your account grows, so grows the amount of the 20%. If you are on a losing streak, the amount of the twenty percent gets smaller, reducing the amount going in until the winning streak starts up again.

Money Management and System/Trade Expectancy

Traders need to keep an edge in order to stay ahead, and not just outperform the market, but to smash it. In the previous section, we took a look at money management tools and concepts. In this section, we'll use those tools and concepts to hone your trading edge and take you one step closer to understanding and using system/trade expectancies effectively.

System/trade expectancy is a process you go through in order to create a firm basis for the probability of your system's long term success. As mentioned in chapter 2, trade expectancy has a formula: expectancy = (probability of win * average win) - (probability of loss * average loss). This formula is implemented in MTS™ from the (winning

UTRENDS
UNIVERSITY

percentage * average % gain)-([1-winning percentage] * average % loss). Up to 90% of MTS™ *MuscleStocks* have positive five-year tested trade expectancy.

In Figure 5.3, Beazer Homes USA Inc (BZH) has a trade expectancy of 11.56% per trade. This means that for every trade made, taking into account the winners and the losers, you would expect to make 11.56% on every trade over time. Since BZH produced 3.3 trades per year, the annual expectancy is 38.43%. This is a ten year test which included two of the worst Bear markets and two of the best Bull markets in history; therefore, the sample size of the test should be sound.

					Please select buy/sell criteria
Back Test	**Equity Curve**	StockSymbol		bzh	
Trade Stats for	**BZH**	Current Signal	Buy		
Number of Trades	34	**Trade expectancy**	$1156.88		☑ **Long**
Total Profit amount	$263,649.81	**Trade expectancy%**	11.56%		
Total Loss amount	$125,543.05	**Annual Trade expectancy**	$3,843.01		Buy / Sell
Total Profit or Total Loss	$138,106.76	**Annual Trade expectancy%**	38.43%		Buy ▾ Sell ▾
Avg Profit on Winners	$13,876.31	**Largest profit**	$105,311.45		
Avg Loss on Losers	$8,369.54	**Largest loss**	$39,839.22		☐ **Short**
Total Net % gain or loss	1381.07%	**Avg days in trade**	58		Sell / Buy
Aver % gain on Winners	29.00%	**Avg days between trades**	54		Sell ▾ Buy ▾
Aver % loss on Losers	10.51%				
Reward to Risk Ratio	2.76				**Investment dollars:** 10000
Number of Trades Per year	3.3				
Number of Winners	19				**Additions on Signals**
Number of Losers	15				☑ **Compound original invesment**
Winning Percentage	55.88				☐ Use fixed amount on new signal
Start date 01/01/2000		**End date** 03/24/2010			Query

Figure 5.3. Beazer Homes USA Inc (BZH) trade statistics showing a total net profit/loss over 1300%, making only 3 trades per year.

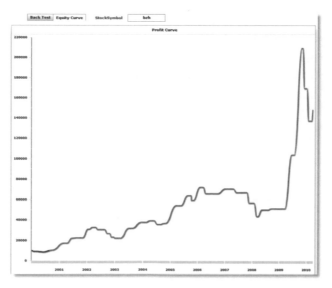

Figure 5.4. Beazer Homes USA Inc (BZH) equity curve.

The examples in Figures 5.3 and 5.4 show the performance of trading a long only strategy on BZH over the past 10 years. The annual trade expectancy is a thirty-eight percent with the average winner being 29% and the average loss of a little more than ten percent. That's a 2.76:1 reward to risk ratio while making three trades a year for ten years. The largest drawdown (peaks to valleys on the profit curve) was 39%.

What could this mean for you going forward? It means that you now have a trading candidate and you can focus on trading this particular stock over and over. Isn't that exciting? You've learned a great deal about the characteristics of this stock and how it reacts to the MTS™ system. This is the kind of stock you want to have and to trade in your watch list.

Here is a look at Google Inc's (GOOG) stat sheet to date (March 24, 2010) since the company's public trading inception (*see* Figures 5.5 and 5.6). The MTS™ system produced twenty trades over this time period, and a 4.3:1 reward to risk ratio, e.g. average gain / average loss = reward to risk ratio, the annual trade expectancy is

29.96%. The reward to risk ratio, annual trade expectancy, and number of trades per year makes Google another stock for the watch list. Even if you only buy two shares, it is a very tradable stock within the system.

| Back Test | Equity Curve | StockSymbol | goog |

Trade Stats for	**GOOG**	Current Signal	Buy			Please select buy/sell criteria
Number of Trades	20	Trade expectancy	$932.21		☑ **Long**	
Total Profit amount	$48,712.92	Trade expectancy%	9.32%		Buy	Sell
Total Loss amount	$11,553.16	Annual Trade expectancy	$3,340.01		Buy ▼	Sell ▼
Total Profit or Total Loss	$37,159.75	Annual Trade expectancy%	33.40%			
Avg Profit on Winners	$4,428.45	Largest profit	$11,976.26			
Avg Loss on Losers	$1,283.68	Largest loss	$3,269.14		☐ **Short**	
Total Net % gain or loss	371.60%	Avg days in trade	62		Sell	Buy
Aver % gain on Winners	20.88%	Avg days between trades	42		Sell ▼	Buy ▼
Aver % loss on Losers	4.81%					
Reward to Risk Ratio	4.34				Investment dollars:	10000
Number of Trades Per year	3.6					
Number of Winners	11				Additions on Signals	
Number of Losers	9				☑ Compound original invesment	
Winning Percentage	55.00				☐ Use fixed amount on new signal	
Start date	08/27/2004	End date	03/24/2010			Query

Figure 5.5. Google Inc (GOOG) long only trade statistics from the first signal on 09/27/2004 through 03/24/2010.

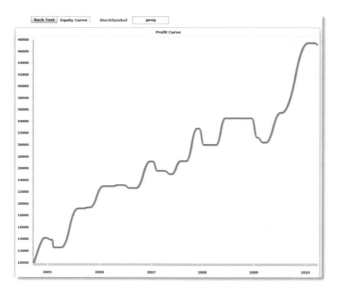

Figure 5.6. Google Inc (GOOG) equity curve showing all activity since its IPO.

So what happens when the trade expectancy isn't exactly panning out? Stop losses can be used in several ways to protect against an extreme move lower. One of the stop loss methods is called the "circus net" stop loss. The idea with the circus net is to set a stop loss well below any area that would be within the stock's reasonable volatility range. The advantage of using the circus net stop loss is that it will stop you out of a trade and protect some of your capital if the stock takes a sharp move lower.

How to Balance Long and Short Positions

Most traders feel like they need to be shorting stocks or always have some short positions "just in case" the market crashes or because if they don't, they aren't considered "real" traders. Many of you may follow newsletter writers whose points of view are always based on very Bearish perspectives. These writers tend to think the world is always coming to an end and you must be positioned appropriately to profit from the end of mankind. What they forget to mention is that you won't be around to enjoy your killing.

Our opinion on balancing long and short positions is that you must know how to short stocks, but even more importantly you must know *when* to short them. A very simple rule of thumb is when MTS™ is signaling a Bullish/Bull market, you should have NO short positions. You're fighting the trend and taking on extreme risk if the stocks you short decide to move significantly higher before finally, if at all, moving lower. Remember from chapter 4 that shorting stocks has *unlimited* upside risk. The conditions for shorting stocks are prime *only* when the MTS™ long term trend signal is in a Bear market. The Bear market signal has been accurate in forecasting further declines in stocks ninety percent of the time in the past 30 years. MTS™ Bear market and Bull market signals are reliable.

How to Protect Against Extreme Downside Moves

If market conditions have started to weaken as indicated by the MTS™ Bearish signal, there are several things to do to protect your gains and principal from significant loss. The first and most basic strategy is to use MTS™ signals and sell your positions on a SELL rating. Stop losses, as discussed previously, are another method of protecting gains and mitigating significant loss if a stock starts to trend lower.

The best way to protect your position is to strictly be in cash if MTS™ has a Bearish/Bear market signal. As of this writing, the last time it had that signal was on January 23, 2008 just before stocks fell apart. To profit from these major moves lower, you can use *put* options as a hedge against holdings you do not or cannot seem to part with. A *put* option provides you with a guaranteed SELL price for specific periods of time, no matter how far a stock's price drops. If you want to cover your position for a longer period of time, you will have to pay for it. Put pricing rises higher as the time period lengthens. Put options are discussed in more detail in *Chapter 8: What are Option Contracts?*

The Reward to Risk Ratio

An equally important money management concept is called the "reward to risk" ratio. This ratio is very important because with the right reward to risk, you can make significant amounts of money, even if you're only right about the direction of the trade forty percent of the time.

The entire approach to trading is built around being correct only forty percent of the time. If we do better, it's a bonus. The MTS™ system provides winning percentages generally between forty and 60% of the time. However, because we only plan on stock winning percentages in the forty to 50% range, we want to make three times as much on the winners as we lose on the losers. In other words, we want a reward to risk ratio of three to one (3:1).

There are some who, upon reading this, will become discouraged with only being right about the direction of the stock forty percent of the time. For those individuals, it is important to understand that there are very few traders who are correct even *half* the time. In fact, if you are 50% on target, you are considered a Wall Street *guru*. Trading systems that may have winning percentages of 80% or higher often have small percentage gains. Whether you are a guru or not, doesn't it make sense to build a trading approach that earns above-average returns? While some methods of prediction may produce fairly accurate results *some of the time*, everyone will benefit from using proven trading methodologies that will perform consistently and make you even more money.

Here's an example that will help illustrate the importance of a good reward to risk ratio. If a trader's system is only right 40% of the time and has a reward to risk ratio of 1:1—meaning for every $1 the trader risks, he can only make one dollar—he will eventually lose all of his trading capital. It doesn't take a math genius to see that if a trader makes $4,000 on four winning trades and loses $6,000 on six losers then he has an overall net loss of two-thousand dollars (-$2,000). This mathematical formula returns negative results. It exemplifies, mathematically, that using 1:1 reward to risk ratio trades leads to a drained account if he is correct forty percent of the time. If a trader wants to set up trades with 1:1 ratios, he will need to be right *sixty percent of the time* to make money (e.g., 6 winners = $6,000; 4 losers = -$4,000; net gain = $2,000).

If the trade has a reward to risk ratio of 2:1, the outcome will be quite different, even being right only 40% of the time. The trader will make $8,000 on four winners and lose six thousand (i.e., -$6,000) on six losers for a net gain of $2,000. This mathematical formula has a positive outcome and will make money every time.

TRENDS
UNIVERSITY

With a 3:1 reward to risk ratio, there would be a $12,000 profit on the four winners and a loss of six thousand dollars on the 6 losers, for a net gain of $6,000. If a trader can determine the direction of the stock 50% of the time, and maintains a 3:1 reward to risk ratio, the results are substantially higher. The trader would make $15,000 on five winning trades and only lose five thousand on 5 losing trades for a net gain of $10,000.

Let's look at a specific example of Apple Inc (AAPL) in Figures 5.7 and 5.8. Starting on January 1, 2000 up until March 24, 2010, Market Trend Signal™ had thirty-eight trades. Seventeen were winners and 21 were losers, giving a forty-five percent winning percentage. The reward to risk for trading this stock over the past ten years has been 3.67:1 on every trade. For those who do not fully understand that incurring losses in trading is completely normal and a part of the cost of trading, this would seem unacceptable.

Back Test	Equity Curve		StockSymbol	aapl	

Trade Stats for	**AAPL**	Current Signal	Buy
Number of Trades	38	Trade expectancy	$868.00
Total Profit amount	$103,019.29	Trade expectancy%	8.68%
Total Loss amount	$33,438.00	Annual Trade expectancy	$3,225.06
Total Profit or Total Loss	$69,581.29	Annual Trade expectancy%	32.25%
Avg Profit on Winners	$6,059.96	Largest profit	$38,733.79
Avg Loss on Losers	$1,592.29	Largest loss	$7,326.43
Total Net % gain or loss	695.81%	Avg days in trade	64
Aver % gain on Winners	29.25%	Avg days between trades	36
Aver % loss on Losers	7.97%		
Reward to Risk Ratio	3.67		
Number of Trades Per year	3.7		
Number of Winners	17		
Number of Losers	21		
Winning Percentage	44.74		

Please select buy/sell criteria

☑ Long
Buy — Sell
Buy ▾ Sell ▾

☐ Short
Sell — Buy
Buy ▾ Sell ▾

Investment dollars: 10000
Additions on Signals:
☑ Compound original invesment
☐ Use fixed amount on new signal

Start date 01/01/2000 📅 End date 03/24/2010 📅

Query

Figure 5.7. Apple Inc (AAPL) trade statistics from 01/01/09 through 03/24/2010.

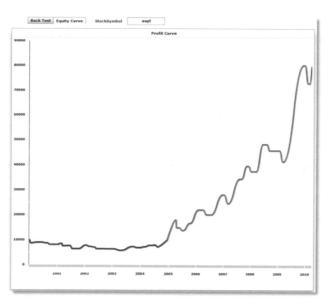

Figure 5.8. Apple Inc (AAPL) equity curve.

In reality, everyone has losing trades. A losing trade doesn't mean you are a failure as a trader. If you look at it as if you are a loser every time you lose money on a trade, you will have a very hard time making money because you will want to hold on to your losing trades in an attempt to prove to yourself that you are right. Ultimately, you will lose your entire trading account. If, on the other hand, you go into your trades planning on being wrong more than you are right but have the right reward to risk ratio, then the losers won't bother you as much and you will consistently be able to make money.

Money Management and Drawdown

Another very important concept of money management is called "drawdown." Drawdown is defined as the peak-to-trough decline during a specific record period of an investment. An easy way to visualize drawdown is to look at the profit curve and then look at the peak to valley movement. From the peak to the valley is the drawdown.

To evaluate the kind of stock you may consider trading, you need to understand its characteristics within the MTS™ system. A critical component of your evaluation is identifying potential stock drawdown.

In the following two examples, the largest drawdown that AAPL experienced was a 23% drop (*see* Figures 5.9 and 5.10). This is certainly an acceptable level of risk you may take in order to get the anticipated reward of hundreds of percentage point gains. In Figures 5.11 and 5.12, Goldman Sachs Group Inc (GS) stocks had a similar experience, although the stock suffered a larger maximum drawdown.

Back Test	Equity Curve	StockSymbol	aapl			Please select buy/sell criteria	

Trade Stats for	**AAPL**	Current Signal	Buy	
Number of Trades	25	Trade expectancy	$1469.13	
Total Profit amount	$155,863.47	Trade expectancy%	14.69%	
Total Loss amount	$42,855.99	Annual Trade expectancy	$5,081.36	
Total Profit or Total Loss	$113,007.47	Annual Trade expectancy%	50.81%	
Avg Profit on Winners	$11,989.50	Largest profit	$59,870.17	
Avg Loss on Losers	$3,571.33	Largest loss	$11,324.34	
Total Net % gain or loss	1130.07%	Avg days in trade	76	
Aver % gain on Winners	35.88%	Avg days between trades	31	
Aver % loss on Losers	8.26%			
Reward to Risk Ratio	4.34			
Number of Trades Per year	3.5			
Number of Winners	13			
Number of Losers	12			
Winning Percentage	52.00			

Please select buy/sell criteria

☑ Long

Buy	Sell
Buy ▾	Sell ▾

☐ Short

Sell	Buy
Buy ▾	Sell ▾

Investment dollars: 10000

Additions on Signals

☑ Compound original invesment
☐ Use fixed amount on new signal

Start date 01/01/2003   End date 03/24/2010

Query

Figure 5.9. Apple Inc (AAPL) trade statistics from 01/01/2003 through 03/24/10 showing an average gain of over thirty-five percent.

Figure 5.10. Apple Inc (AAPL) equity curve showing typical drawdown from 2003.

Back Test	Equity Curve	StockSymbol	gs			
Trade Stats for	**GS**		Current Signal	Buy		Please select buy/sell criteria

Number of Trades	29	Trade expectancy	$365.38		☑ Long	
Total Profit amount	$29,478.76	Trade expectancy%	3.65%		Buy	Sell
Total Loss amount	$16,120.05	Annual Trade expectancy	$1,464.57			
Total Profit or Total Loss	$13,358.71	Annual Trade expectancy%	14.65%		Buy ▾	Sell ▾
Avg Profit on Winners	$1,734.04	Largest profit	$6,525.02			
Avg Loss on Losers	$1,343.34	Largest loss	$4,300.87		☐ Short	
Total Net % gain or loss	133.59%	Avg days in trade	55		Sell	Buy
Aver % gain on Winners	10.95%	Avg days between trades	35			
Aver % loss on Losers	6.68%				Buy ▾	Sell ▾
Reward to Risk Ratio	1.64					
Number of Trades Per year	4.0				Investment dollars:	10000
Number of Winners	17					
Number of Losers	12				Additions on Signals	
Winning Percentage	58.62				☑ Compound original invesment	
					☐ Use fixed amount on new signal	
Start date	01/01/2003	End date	03/24/2010			Query

Figure 5.11. Trade statistics for Goldman Sachs Group Inc (GS) showing trade expectancy from 2003.

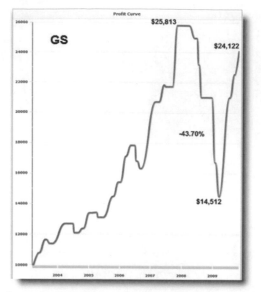

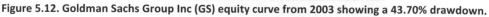

Figure 5.12. Goldman Sachs Group Inc (GS) equity curve from 2003 showing a 43.70% drawdown.

On the trade of Freeport McMoRan Copper & Gold Inc (FCX) in Figures 5.13 through 5.15, the stock dropped over 81% but the equity curve was down only nineteen and a quarter percentage points. The same stock was traded over and over again which resulted in the growth of the investor's account to nearly 100% over the last equity curve high, while the stock had yet to reach previous highs of $130.

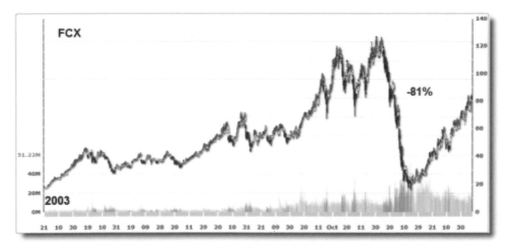

Figure 5.13. Freeport McMoRan Copper & Gold Inc (FCX) trade signals since 2003.

Trade Stats for	**FCX**	Current Signal	Buy
Number of Trades	24	Trade expectancy	$1075.72
Total Profit amount	$77,052.28	Trade expectancy%	10.75%
Total Loss amount	$26,858.09	Annual Trade expectancy	$3,569.75
Total Profit or Total Loss	$50,194.19	Annual Trade expectancy%	35.70%
Avg Profit on Winners	$6,421.02	Largest profit	$17,819.06
Avg Loss on Losers	$2,238.17	Largest loss	$9,003.00
Total Net % gain or loss	501.94%	Avg days in trade	73
Aver % gain on Winners	27.90%	Avg days between trades	40
Aver % loss on Losers	6.39%		
Reward to Risk Ratio	4.37		
Number of Trades Per year	3.3		
Number of Winners	12		
Number of Losers	12		
Winning Percentage	50.00		

Back Test | Equity Curve   StockSymbol | fcx

Please select buy/sell criteria

☑ Long

Buy | Sell
Buy ▼ | Sell ▼

☐ Short

Sell | Buy
Buy ▼ | Sell ▼

Investment dollars: 10000

Additions on Signals

☑ Compound original invesment
☐ Use fixed amount on new signal

Query

Start date 01/01/2003   End date 03/24/2010

Figure 5.14. Freeport McMoRan Copper & Gold Inc (FCX) trade statistics from 2003.

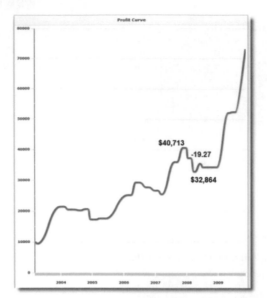

Figure 5.15. Freeport McMoRan Copper & Gold Inc (FCX) equity curve from 2003.

To summarize, I hope you're starting to see a common theme throughout this book. The system generates about three to 4 long trades per year (double that for long/short strategies). Real wealth is generated in compounding gains over time—not in short-term active trading. And the time you save to actually enjoy your life is priceless.

Notes and Comments

Notes and Comments

Market Trend Signal™
Market Timing - Trend Following - Stock Ratings

Chapter 6
Price and Retracement Patterns in Trend Following

Contents

Stocks in an upward trend will eventually have a pull back. These pull backs are also known as *retracements, countertrends, consolidations, bases, corrections, ABC patterns* and in the world of trading, many other names. These names fit the descriptions of what each trend pattern indicates—the price of the stock simply takes a break or pauses from the upward trend. These corrections may be quick or they can last a while. Their tell-tale patterns or shapes graphically display market corrections. In this chapter, I will discuss the most common of these patterns with you.

Identifying Trends with Patterns

The MTS™ system is designed to trade the trends not the corrections, so you will see most Buy rated stocks moving up at an angle starting from the lower left and climbing toward the upper right on the price chart. The Sell rated stocks move down from the upper left toward the lower right. Most Hold rated patterns are doing neither...they appear steady, not moving in either direction.

Hold rated stocks can be in transition from an upward trend to a down trend or they move from DN (down) to UP. The chart may also show you that the stock has *paused* in its movement. The purpose of this chapter is to help you visually understand what is taking place during the Hold rating.

Countertrend ABC Patterns

Countertrend moves in the MTS™ system are almost always HOLD. For example, sometimes you will see a stock that is in a Buy rated up trend then it goes to a HOLD correction that dips into the SELL for a short time before it moves back to HOLD and then continues the Buy rated upward trend.

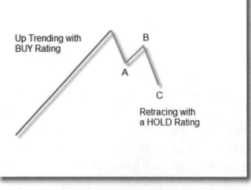

Figure 6.1. Upward trend with Buy rating falling in value (A), ascending upward often called a "suckers rally" (B), then retracing with a Hold rating (C).

TRENDS UNIVERSITY

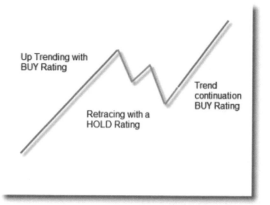

Up Trending with
BUY Rating

Trend
continuation
BUY Rating

Retracing with a
HOLD Rating

Figure 6.2. Upward trend with Buy rating retracing with a continuous Hold rating during the correction, continuing the upward trend to trigger a Buy rating. When you see a HOLD rating the stock is pausing. Watch it and prepare for the next move.

Figure 6.3. iShares COMEX Gold Trust (IAU) stock chart displaying retracements in an upward trend, gradually climbing to $106.

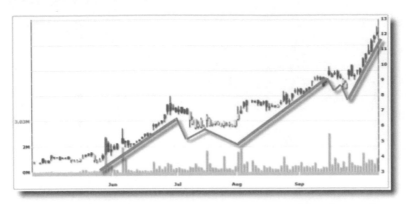

Figure 6.4. Candlestick stock chart displaying retracements in an upward trend over a four month period.

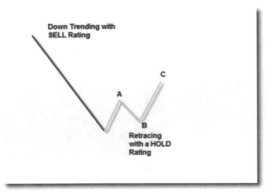

Figure 6.5. Descending trend with Sell rating, ascending upward (A), retracing to a Hold rating (B), then ascending upward (C).

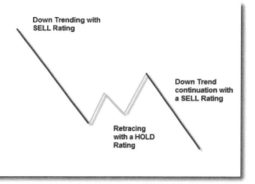

Figure 6.6. Bearish pattern beginning in a downward trend with a Sell rating, ascending with two successive Hold ratings, continuing upward, and finally turning downward, triggering a Sell rating.

Figure 6.7. Goldman Sachs Group Inc (GS) candlestick chart displaying Bearish retracement patterns with successive Hold ratings.

129

Analyzing Trends Using Familiar Patterns

The Cup Pattern

The "cup with handle" pattern shown in Figure 6.8 indicates that there is a Bullish continuation pattern. The pattern marks a consolidation period followed by a breakout. It was developed by William O'Neil who introduced this concept in his 1988 book entitled <u>How to Make Money in Stocks: A Winning System in Good Times and Bad</u> (O'Neil, 1988).

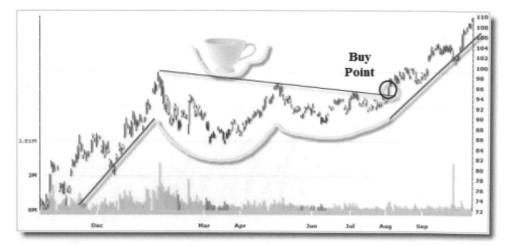

Figure 6.8. Stock chart indicating a "cup with handle" pattern.

As the pattern's name implies, there are two parts to the pattern: the cup and the handle. The cup forms after an advance and looks like a bowl or cup with a rounded bottom. As the cup is completed, a trading range develops on the right hand side which forms the handle. A subsequent breakout from the handle's trading range signals a continuation of the prior advance.

The Cup Continuation Pattern

U TRENDS
UNIVERSITY

To qualify as a continuation pattern, a prior trend should exist. Ideally, the trend should be a few months old and not too mature. The more mature the trend, the less chance that the pattern will mark a continuation or the less upside potential it will have.

The Cup Shape

The cup should be "U" shaped and resemble a bowl or cup with a rounded bottom. A "V" shaped bottom would be considered too sharp of a reversal to qualify. The softer "U" shape ensures that the cup is a consolidation pattern with valid support that is round at the bottom. The perfect pattern would have equal highs on both sides of the cup, but this is not always the case.

Depth of the Cup

Ideally, the depth of the cup should retrace one-third (1/3) or less of the previous advance. However, with volatile markets and over-reactions, the retracement could range from 1/3 to one half. In extreme situations, the maximum retracement could be two thirds of the previous advance.

The Cup Handle

After the high forms on the right side of the cup, there is a pull back that forms the handle. Sometimes this handle resembles a flag or pennant that slopes downward, other times just a short pull back will produce a short handle. The handle represents the final consolidation/pull back before the big breakout. It can retrace up to one-third (1/3) of the cup's advance, but usually not more. The smaller the retracement is, the more Bullish the formation and more significant the breakout. Sometimes it is prudent to wait for a break above the resistance line which is established by the highs of the cup.

The Cup Duration

The formation of the cup can last from one to 6 months, and sometimes longer on weekly charts. The cup's handle typically forms over the duration of a single week to many weeks, and ideally completes its formation within a one to four week time period.

Cup Volume

There should be a substantial increase in volume on the breakout above the handle's resistance.

The Cup's Projected Advance (Target)

The projected advance or "essence of the pattern" after breakout can be estimated by measuring the distance from the right peak of the cup to the bottom of the cup. As with most chart patterns, determining the projected advance or "target" is more important to capture than the particulars. Instead, use the particulars of the cup's shape to more clearly estimate the *advance* or target.

Triangles, Flags and Pennants

Ascending Triangles

Ascending triangles will mark a variation of the symmetrical triangle and are generally considered Bullish. These shapes are most reliable when found in an upward trend. The top part of the triangle appears flat, while the bottom part of the triangle has an upward slant. If the chart is showing an ascending triangle, the market typically becomes overbought and prices are turned back. Then buying re-enters the market and prices soon reach their old highs, where they are once again turned back. Buying then resurfaces, although at a higher level than before. Prices eventually break through the old highs and are propelled even higher as new buying comes in. Buy ratings can take place before or after the upper line and usually happen very near the uppermost location.

Figure 6.9. Candlestick stock chart displaying ascending triangle patterns in an upward trend.

Symmetrical Triangles

Symmetrical triangles can be characterized as areas of indecision—the time when a market pauses and future direction is questioned. Typically, the forces of supply and demand at that moment are considered nearly equal. Attempts to push higher are quickly met by selling, while dips are seen as bargains. Each new lower top and higher bottom becomes more shallow than the last, taking on the shape of a sideways triangle. While this is happening, there is a tendency for volume to diminish. Eventually, this indecision is met with resolve and usually explodes out of this formation—often on heavy volume. Symmetrical triangles overwhelmingly resolve themselves in the direction of the trend.

Flags and Pennants

Flags and pennants can also be categorized as continuation patterns. They usually represent only brief pauses in a trending market. They're typically seen right after a big, quick move after which the market usually takes off again in the same direction. These

patterns are some of the most reliable continuation patterns used to determine projected advances.

Figure 6.10. Medifast Inc (MED) chart displaying symmetrical triangles and flags and pennants in an upward trend.

Bullish flags are characterized by lower tops and lower bottoms, with the pattern slanting against the trend. But unlike wedges, their trend lines run parallel. Bearish flags are comprised of higher tops and higher bottoms. Bear flags also have a tendency to slope against the trend. Both Bullish and Bearish trend lines run parallel. Pennants look very much like symmetrical triangles, except pennants are typically smaller in size (based on volatility) and are shorter in duration.

Notes and Comments

Notes and Comments

Notes and Comments

Chapter 7
Candlestick Charts Explained

Contents

The History of Candlestick Charts

Candlestick charts are on record as being the oldest type of charts used for price prediction. They date back to the 1700s when they were used for predicting rice prices. In fact, during this era in Japan, Munehisa Homma became a legendary rice trader and gained a huge fortune using candlestick analysis. He is said to have executed over one hundred consecutive winning trades!

What Do Candlesticks Look Like?

Candlestick charts are much more visually appealing than a standard two-dimensional bar chart. As in a standard bar chart, there are four elements necessary to construct a candlestick chart: the open, high, low and closing price for a given time period. Below are examples of candlesticks and a definition for each candlestick component.

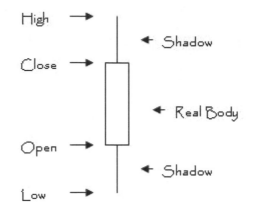

Figure 7.1. A typical candlestick with callouts to each element/component. The open real body indicates a gain in the stock's value at the close of the day's trading.

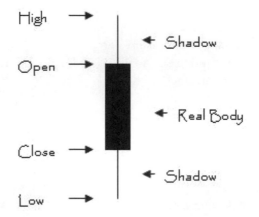

Figure 7.2. A typical candlestick with callouts to each element/component. The solid real body indicates a loss in the stock's value at the close of the day's trading.

The body of the candlestick is called the "real body" and represents the range between the opening and closing prices. A down day or filled-in real body represents that the close during that time period was lower than the open which is normally considered Bearish. When the real body is open or "up day," it means that the close was higher than the open which is normally Bullish. The thin vertical line above and/or below the real body is called the "upper/lower shadow," representing the high/low price extremes for the period.

The lines above and below the body are called "shadows." Shadows represent the session's price extremes. The shadow above the real body is called the "upper" shadow and the shadow below the real body is called the "lower" shadow. The top of the upper shadow is the high of the day and the bottom of the lower shadow is the low of the day.

One of the main differences between the western line and the Japanese candlestick line is the relationship between open and closing prices. A western viewpoint places the greatest importance on the closing price of a stock in relation to the prior period's close. Japanese investors, by comparison, place the highest importance on the close as it relates to the open of the same day. You can see why the Japanese candlestick line and its highly graphical representation of the open to close relationship is such an indispensable tool for traders.

A Note about Candlestick Color

Candlesticks in basic charting tools traditionally use either white or green to show an up day and black or red to show a down day. The color of the candlestick is irrelevant to the analysis, but the color makes it easier to detect where opening and closing prices are relative to each other for that day. If the open is higher than the close, the candlestick body is shown as white or green; if the close is lower than the open, the candlestick body is black or red.

In the MTS™ system, the color of the candle references the current signal of the stock relative to BUY, HOLD or SELL signals as opposed to referencing a stock's performance for the trading day. In this chapter, we explain candlestick formations using traditional coloring that you may find on basic charting tools. Remember that we are concerned

only about the "formation" of the candlestick pattern, not whether the stock has an up or down day.

Candlestick Charts vs. Western Bar Charts

The western bar chart is made up of four components: open, high, low, and close. The vertical bar displays the high and low of the session, the left horizontal line represents the open, and the right horizontal line represents the close.

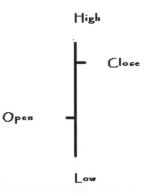

Figure 7.3. Western bar chart line displaying standard elements.

Common Candlestick Terminology

The following is a list of some individual candlestick terms and formations.

The Down Day Candlestick

The down day candlestick (*see* Figure 7.4) is used to show when the close is lower than the open.

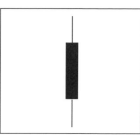

Figure 7.4. A down day candlestick can be green, yellow or red in the MTS™ system.

The UP Day Candlestick

An up day candlestick (*see* Figure 7.5) is shown when the close is higher than the open.

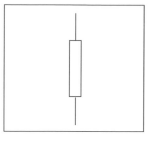

Figure 7.5. An up day candlestick can be green, yellow or red in the MTS™ system.

The "Shaven Head" Candlestick

The "shaven head" candlestick shown in Figure 7.6 is a candlestick with no upper shadow. The absence of an upper shadow indicates that the price at the close of the day's trading is the uppermost or highest price for the day's performance.

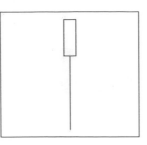

Figure 7.6. A "shaven head" candlestick.

The "Shaven Bottom" Candlestick.

The "shaven bottom" candlestick (*see* Figure 7.7) has no lower shadow, indicating the lowermost or lowest price of a stock's performance for the day.

Figure 7.7. A "shaven bottom" candlestick.

Spinning Tops

The "spinning top" candlestick shown in Figure 7.8 has a small real body. When these appear within a sideways choppy market, they represent equilibrium between the Bulls and the Bears. They can be either up day or down day.

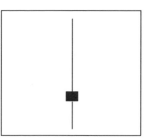

Figure 7.8. A "spinning top" candlestick.

Doji Lines

Doji lines have no real body (*see* Figure 7.9). They are depicted on the chart with a horizontal line when the open and close of a stock's price are the same or very close. The length of the shadow can vary.

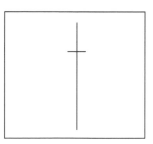

Figure 7.9. A Doji line.

Candlestick Reversal Patterns

Just as many traders look to bar charts for double tops and bottoms, head-and-shoulders, and other technical indicators for reversal signals, so too can candlestick formations be examined for the same purpose. A reversal does not always mean that the current up or down trend will reverse direction, but merely that the current direction may end. The market may decide to drift sideways.

Candlestick reversal patterns must be viewed within the context of prior activity to be effective. In fact, identical candlesticks may have different meanings, depending on where they occur within the context of prior trends and formations. When used in conjunction with trend following analyses, candlestick patterns give additional confirmation that the trend pattern may be showing signs of continuation or reversal.

In this section, we'll cover examples of candlestick reversal patterns that that will help you identify upward and downward trends.

The "candlestick hammer" or "the hammer" of a candlestick is the key to determining the context of a down trend. Its appearance (*see* Figures 7.10 through 7.12) has a long lower shadow with a small real body. The shadow should be at least twice the length of the real body. There should be a very small or non-existent upper shadow. The candlestick body may be either down day or up day because a hammer can be present regardless of whether the stock finished above or below the day's open or close. The presence of a hammer means that the market may be "hammering" out a bottom.

Let's take a look at a couple of examples for the candlestick hammer.

Figure 7.10. The "hammer" candlestick.

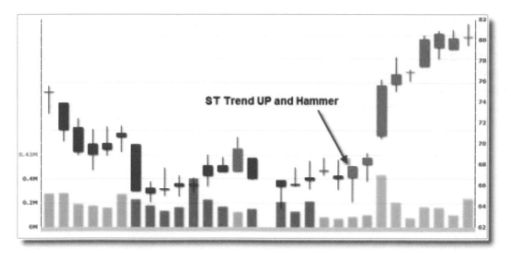

Figure 7.11. The "hammer" candlestick is used to support reversal patterns for ST up trends.

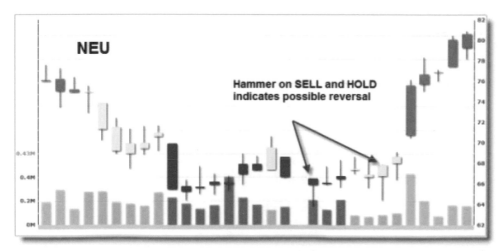

Figure 7.12. The "hammer" candlestick is used to support reversal patterns for SELL and HOLD signals.

The "Hanging Man" Candlestick

The "hanging man" is identical in appearance to the *hammer*, but appears within the context of an upward trend (*see* Figures 7.13 and 7.14). It is used to determine the context of a market that is trending upward, but is an indication of a possible weakening trend.

Figure 7.13. The "hanging man" candlestick.

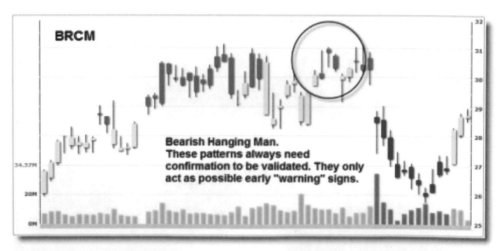

Figure 7.14. A Bearish "hanging man" indicating a reversal pattern for BRCM acting as an early warning sign for a possible down trend.

Engulfing Candlestick Patterns

Engulfing patterns are effective visuals that indicate strong possibilities of trend reversals. There are two types of engulfing patterns: *Bullish* and *Bearish*. Keep in mind that both types of engulfing patterns must be located and affirmed by a market that is in a *definable* trend—not chopping around sideways. The shadows of the prior candlestick in either instance do not need to be engulfed.

In Figures 7.15 through 7.17, examples of a Bullish engulfing patterns are shown as up day real bodies that completely cover or "engulf" the prior day's real body.

Figure 7.15. The Bullish engulfing pattern.

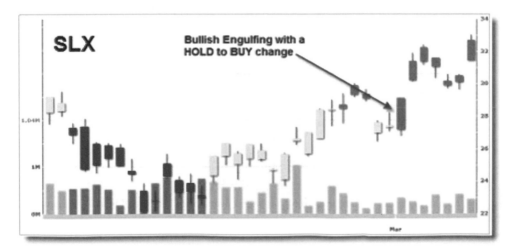

Figure 7.16. Bullish engulfing pattern with a HOLD to BUY signal.

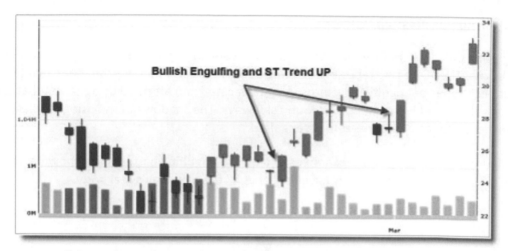

Figure 7.17. Bullish engulfing pattern with the ST trend rising upward.

A Bearish engulfing pattern appears as a down day candlestick real body that totally covers or "engulfs" the prior day's real body (*see* Figures 7.18 and 7.19).

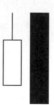

Figure 7.18. An up day candlestick (left) of previous day's real body being engulfed by a down day candlestick (right).

Figure 7.19. A Bearish solid candlestick engulfs the previous day's real body indicating a possible reversal pattern for a downward trend.

The Bearish "dark-cloud cover" reversal pattern applies to Bearish markets where a top reversal formation from the first day of the pattern consists of a strong, up day real body (*see* Figure 7.20). The second day's price opens above the top of the upper shadow of the prior candlestick, but the close is at or near the low of the day, and well into the prior up day real body.

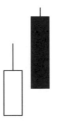

Figure 7.20. Bearish "dark-cloud cover" reversal pattern showing top reversal formation.

Piercing Candlestick Patterns

Piercing patterns apply to Bullish markets and are just the opposite of the *dark-cloud cover* pattern. These occur within a market that is trending downward (*see* Figure 7.21). The first candlestick has a down day real body and the second has a long, up day real body. The up day opens sharply lower and below the low of the prior down day. Then, prices close above the 50% point of the prior day's down day real body.

Figure 7.21. A Bullish market piercing pattern showing a market that is trending downward. The piercing day may be an indication of a pending trend reversal.

The "Harami" Candlestick Pattern

The word "Harami" is a Japanese word that essentially means "pregnant." The shape of this candlestick pattern resembles a pregnant mother (*see* Figure 7.22). The Harami pattern is a reversal pattern. In Figure 7.23, we can see that after a significant Bearish day, the stock gaps open to a higher price without much movement in relation to the opening price. After a strong day of selling, the reversal pattern indicates that the period for selling is subsiding. A trader would ideally like to see another Bullish day of follow-through for additional confirmation of a Bullish trade.

Figure 7.22. Harami candles gap higher than the previous day's close and trade within a close range for the day. The Harami shows a lack of buyer and seller interest.

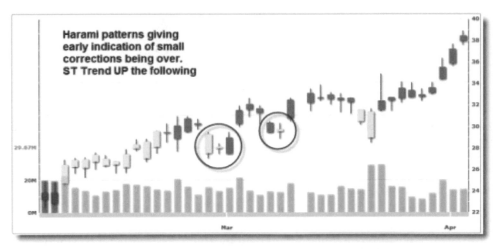

Figure 7.23. Bullish Harami patterns are reversal indicators. The ST Trend UP signal in this example gives additional Bullish confirmation. The green Buy signal confirms the pattern as an early trend reversal.

The Bullish Harami pattern in Figures 7.24 and 7.25 shows a very strong down day with no additional buying or selling the next day as a follow-through. This indicates that the Bearish demand may be slowing, at least in the short term. If this pattern is at the top of a long rally, it is more Bearish than if it is found at the beginning of a possible upward trend.

Figure 7.24. Bearish Harami candlestick pattern indicating a possible reversal of the upward trend.

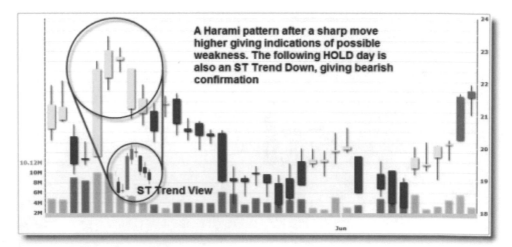

Figure 7.25. Bearish Harami patterns can be an early warning of a trend that is slowing. The Hold signal turns to SELL a few days after the pattern is shown.

Star Candlestick Patterns

Stars are the equivalent of gaps on standard bar charts. Star candlesticks have four separate reversal patterns, each having its own name. The four are listed here are the *Morning* star, the *Evening* star, the *Doji* star, and the *Shooting Star* which is also known as the *Inverted Hammer.*

Overall, star candlestick formations consist of a small real body gapping above or below the preceding day's real body. The real body of the star should not overlap the prior real body. The color of the star or its location is not too important. Star formations can occur at either tops or bottoms of trends. Stars are the equivalent of gaps on standard bar charts.

Let's take a closer look at the star reversal patterns.

The Morning Star. Morning stars create a Bullish bottom-reversal pattern. The formation consists of three candlesticks. The first candlestick is a tall down day real body followed by the second, smaller real body that gaps or opens lower, forming the star pattern. The third candlestick is an up day real body that moves well into the first period's down day real body (*see* Figure 7.26). This is similar to an island pattern on standard bar charts.

Figure 7.26. The star gaps lower than the previous trading day then has little price movement. The small price movement is followed by a strong move higher, often accompanied by an ST Trend UP signal.

The Evening Star. Evening stars create a Bearish top-reversal pattern and are counterpart to the Morning star. In Figure 7.27, we can see that three candlesticks comprise the Evening star, the first being long and up day. The second forms the star followed by the third candlestick, which has a down day real body that moves sharply into the first up day candlestick.

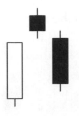

Figure 7.27. The star gaps higher than the previous close and has little price movement. The third candle is a sharp move down. This candle is often accompanied by an ST Trend DN (down) signal.

<u>**Doji Stars**</u>. When a star gaps above a real body in an up trend, or gaps under a real body in a falling market, it is called a "Doji" star. Two popular Doji stars are known as the *Evening Doji* star and the *Morning Doji* star (*see* Figure 7.28).

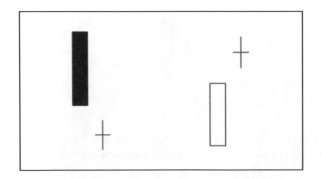

Figure 7.28. A Morning Doji star (left) compared to an Evening Doji star (right). Translated into English, Doji means "indecision." These are days when the stock may start out with a strong move, but indecision as to direction sets in.

The Evening Doji star is a Doji star in an upward trend followed by a long, down day real body that closed well into the prior up day real body (*see* Figures 7.29). If the candlestick after the Doji star has gapped higher versus lower (as shown), the Bearishness of the

Doji is invalidated. In Figure 7.30, MTS™ had a HOLD rating during the Doji pattern, also confirming that caution in buying the new rally was warranted.

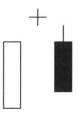

Figure 7.29. The Evening Doji star shown gapping away from previous up day followed by sharp down day.

Figure 7.30. The Evening Doji star indicates weakness in the stock during the Bullish attempt higher. The down day after the Doji confirms the Bearishness of the pattern.

The Morning Doji star is a Doji star in a downward trend followed by a long up day real body that closes well into the prior down day real body (*see* Figures 7.31 and 7.32). If the candlestick after the Doji star has gapped higher, the Bearishness of the Doji is invalidated.

Figure 7.31. The Morning Doji star signaling a potential stall or reversal of the down trend.

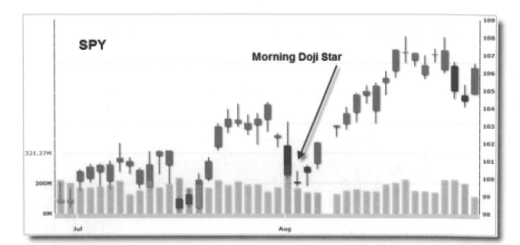

Figure 7.32. Morning Dojis by themselves only indicate indecision. They still need a confirming up day on the next candle to offer an actual signal.

The Shooting Star. In Figure 7.33, the Shooting Star is a small real body near the lower end of the trading range, with a long upper shadow. The color of the body is not critical. The appearance of this star does not usually indicate a major reversal sign, only a warning. A stalling trend is indicated with the Shooting Star in Figure 7.34.

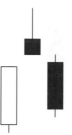

Figure 7.33. The Shooting Star candlestick pattern. The Shooting Star is similar to other stars but its presence indicates a very volatile day with a lot of price movement.

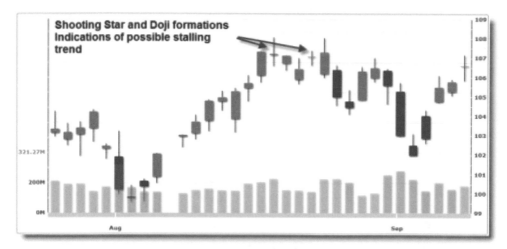

Figure 7.34. Shooting Star and Doji formations indicating possible stalling trend.

The Inverted Hammer. The Inverted Hammer shown in Figure 7.35 is not really a star, but does look like a Shooting Star. When occurring within a down trend, as seen in Figure 7.36, the appearance of an Inverted Hammer may signal a turning market. The color of the candlestick body is not critical.

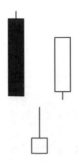

Figure 7.35. An Inverted Hammer candlestick pattern. The presence of an Inverted Hammer can be a strong reversal signal when confirmation is given the following day.

Figure 7.36. The Inverted Hammer pattern. The ST Trend UP signal is given on the first day after the pattern.

Notes and Comments

Notes and Comments

Notes and Comments

Chapter 8
What are Option Contracts?

Contents

continued

Contents continued

An option contract is an agreement between two parties to buy or sell a stock at a fixed price on a predetermined date. There are two types of option contracts: *call* options and *put* options. A call option gives the buyer the right to *buy* underlying stock, while a put option gives the buyer the right to *sell* underlying stock. The contract is called an "option" contract because the buyer is not obligated to carry out the transaction. If, for example, the stock value decreases over the life of the contract, the buyer can simply elect not to exercise his or her right to buy or sell the stock.

The value of the stock which is stated in the agreement is referred to as the "exercise" or "strike" price. This is the price at which the stock will be exchanged. The date of purchase is known as the "expiration" or "maturity" date. This date is the deadline for the option contract. The option buyer decides if the transaction will occur on this date.

Let's look at a quick example of a call option which gives Jerry the right to buy underlying stock. Jerry buys a call option contract from Jane. The terms of the option contract states that Jerry will buy 100 shares of Apple Inc (AAPL) on May 5th of this year for a fixed price of $25 (strike price).

Why would Jerry want to use a call option? The option contract is attractive because AAPL is doing well and stands to increase in value if the trend continues upward. The predetermined date on the contract is close enough to take a calculated risk that the value will continue to rise to $30 or higher, for example, giving Jerry a strong probability of gaining at least five dollars on the transaction.

Let's say that the share price of AAPL is trading above $25 on the expiration day—the predetermined date of May 5. Jerry decides to exercise his right to buy the stock and Jane must sell him the shares for the agreed amount of $25. Jerry would realize his profit by selling those shares on the open market for the current share price. If the current share price of AAPL is $30, then a simple math calculation shows that he will take a five dollar profit.

Alternatively, if AAPL is trading at $20, then buying the shares from Jane at $25 makes no financial sense. He can just as easily buy the stock on the open market at $20. In this situation, Jerry would choose not to exercise his right to buy the shares and let the option contract expire worthless. His only loss would be the amount that he paid to Jane when he bought the contract, which is called the "option premium"—more on that a little later. Jane would, however, keep the option premium received from Jerry as her profit.

In the real world of exchange-traded options, transactions don't really take place between two individuals like I've explained above. The process of novation actually removes identities of both parties. Novation is the process undertaken by a clearing house, whereby it substitutes itself between the buyer and the seller of a trade, and acts as the "middleman" to guarantee the obligations of each party. The trader simply buys or sells an option contract from the exchange without knowing who is on the other side.

Options Pricing and Premiums

The premium of an option has two main components: intrinsic value and extrinsic or "time" value. Both the intrinsic and extrinsic value of a stock option make up the price of option contracts.

The intrinsic value is determined by the price of the underlying stock at any given time. Intrinsic value is the current stock price minus the strike price. The extrinsic value is determined by other factors. The longer the amount of time for market conditions to work to an investor's benefit, the greater the extrinsic or time value. Extrinsic value is the option premium minus the intrinsic value.

In Table 8.1, we've made a quick reference to calculate premium pricing and options intrinsic and extrinsic pricing.

Intrinsic Value	
	Current Stock Price - Strike Price
Extrinsic (Time) Value	
	Option Premium - Intrinsic Value
Option Premium	
	Intrinsic Value + Extrinsic Value

Table 8.1. Quick reference calculations.

Intrinsic Value

An option's intrinsic value is determined by the value of the option contract's underlying stock. An option's premium is also affected by the value of the underlying stock using the same guideline. The purpose of this section is to define intrinsic value calls and puts.

Intrinsic Value of Calls and Puts

A *call* has intrinsic value when the value of an option contract's underlying stock is *higher* than the strike price. The call owner could exercise his right to buy stock shares if the price of the underlying stock rises higher than the strike price of the call option, or simply sell the call option before expiration. Therefore, buying a call option is a Bullish strategy.

A *put* has intrinsic value when the stock's price is *lower* than the strike price. A put option gives the option buyer the right to sell a certain number of shares of stock at a specific price on or before a specific date. If the put buyer decides to exercise his right, the put seller is legally obligated to buy the shares from the seller. If you recall in chapter 4, good examples of Bearish strategies are shorting stocks or buying put options.

The difference between a call and put option contract is how it is used: a long *call* option is a Bullish strategy (I expect the stock to go up), while a long *put* option is a Bearish strategy (I expect the stock to go down).

It's about the Money

"In the Money" (ITM). A call option is "in the money" (ITM) if the price of the underlying stock is higher than the option's contract strike price. Conversely, a put option is ITM if the price of the underlying stock is lower than the option's contract strike price.

"Out of the Money" (OTM). A call option is "out of the money" (OTM) if the price of the underlying stock is below the option's contract strike price. Conversely, a put option is OTM if the price of the underlying stock is higher than the option's contract strike price.

"At the Money" (ATM). "At the money" options can be either ITM or OTM. They are simply the closest strike price to the current market value of the stock.

If a stock is trading at or near the strike price, the strike price is considered to be ATM. When a stock is trading below the strike price of a call option or above the strike price of a put option, the strike is considered to be OTM. When a stock is trading above the strike price of a call option or below the strike price of a put option, the strike is considered to be ITM. These concepts will be repeated throughout this chapter.

Only ITM options have intrinsic value, representing the difference between the current price of the underlying stock and the option's exercise (strike) price. A *call* option is said to be "in the money" because its value is *above* the strike price. A *put* option is also said to the "in the money" but only if the stock's price is *below* the strike price.

Extrinsic Value

Prior to the expiration date of an option, any premium in excess of intrinsic value is called "extrinsic value" or "time value." Extrinsic value is also defined as the amount an investor is willing to pay for an option *above* its intrinsic value. Traders look for extrinsic value in the hope that at some time prior to expiration, changes in the price of the underlying stock will increase the option's value.

The longer the amount of time for market conditions to work to an investor's benefit, the greater the option's extrinsic value. If you want to cover your position for a longer period of time, you will have to pay for it. Put pricing rises higher as the time period to expiration lengthens.

Five Major Factors Influencing an Option's Premium

There are five major factors that influence option premiums. The factors having the greatest effect are:

1. Changes in the price of underlying stock,
2. Strike price,
3. Time until expiration,
4. Volatility of underlying stock, and
5. Dividends/Risk-free interest rates.

Changes in the Underlying Stock Price

Changes in the underlying stock price can increase or decrease the value of an option. These price changes have opposite effects on calls and puts. For instance, as the value of the underlying stock rises, a call will generally increase and the value of a put will generally decrease in price. A decrease in the underlying stock's value will generally have the opposite effect.

The Strike Price Factor

The strike price determines whether or not an option has any intrinsic value. An option's premium (intrinsic value plus extrinsic value) generally increases as the option becomes further "in the money," and decreases as the option becomes more deeply "out of the money."

Time Until Expiration

The time until expiration affects the time value component of an option's premium. Generally, as expiration approaches, the levels of an option's time value for puts and calls decreases or erodes. This effect is most noticeable with "at the money" options.

Volatility of Underlying Stocks

The effect of volatility is the most subjective and perhaps the most difficult factor to quantify, but it can have a significant impact on the time value portion of an option's premium. Volatility is simply a measure of risk (uncertainty), or variability of price of an option's underlying stock. Higher volatility estimates reflect greater expected fluctuations in either direction in underlying price levels. This expectation generally results in higher option premiums for puts and calls alike, and is most noticeable with at-the-money options. This is often referred to as *Implied Volatility* and is taught in detail in our DVD courses at www.TrendsUniversity.com.

Dividends/Risk-Free Interest Rates

The interest rate on a three-month U.S. Treasury bill is often used as the risk-free rate. These interest rates have less impact to the value of premiums.

Why Trade Options?

Option trading provides some advantages over other trading investment vehicles. Some advantages are leverage, limited risk, insurance, and profiting in Bear markets. This is

the short list containing only a few advantages traders use to benefit from trading options. In this section, we'll take a look at some examples of these advantages.

There are a few things to know about buyers, sellers and the nature of buying option contracts before we continue. As I mentioned earlier, an option contract is an agreement where the buyer has the option to decide if a transaction is to take place. When the buyer enters into an options contract, he (or she) pays an amount known as an "option premium" to the option seller. The option premium is the amount paid by the buyer to enter into the contract.

An option seller is also known as the "writer" of the option. When a buyer enters into a contract with the writer, the buyer is buying the right but not the obligation to buy the stock in the future at a certain price—no stock is actually transferred until the buyer chooses to exercise the option. The value of the contract is determined by the price of the underlying stock and other factors as discussed earlier.

Leverage

Leverage is the main tool used by traders to get larger returns using less money. Once an option contract is executed, the terms in the contract give buyers the right to buy a specific number of shares of the underlying stock. The amount of shares to buy is determined by the number of option contracts multiplied by the contract multiplier. The contract multiplier which is also called "contract size" is different for most classes of options and is determined by each exchange.

In the United States, the contract size for options on shares is one hundred (100). In other words, a single option contract (one contract) gives you the right to buy 100 shares of stock from the option seller. So, let's say that you buy ten IBM option contracts. You own the right to buy 1,000 IBM shares at expiration (e.g., 10 x 100 = 1000). You would consider exercising your option if the price of IBM was trading higher than the strike price of the IBM option you purchased.

Continuing with this example, the price of the option is also multiplied by the contract multiplier. You decide to purchase 10 IBM options contracts which equates to a thousand shares that are quoted in the marketplace for $1.50 each. To buy the option contract you would pay the seller or "writer" $1,500.

This is a crucial concept to understand. If you buy five IBM share options (instead of ten) for $1.50 that have a strike price of $25, then you will pay the option seller seven hundred and fifty dollars (e.g., 5 x 100 = 500 x 1.50 = $750). If you decide to exercise your right and buy the shares, you will have to buy five hundred, e.g. 5 x 100 shares (one hundred being the contract size) at the exercise price of $25 each, which will cost you $12,500.

The bottom line is that your initial investment of seven hundred and fifty dollars has given you $12,500 exposure in the underlying stock. This is called "leverage" which effectively gives you opportunities to utilize a very large exposure while only outlaying a small amount of capital up front. For obvious reasons, using leverage with stock option contracts appeals to the small investor.

Let's say you bought a twenty-five dollar call option for $1 while the underlying stock shares were trading at $26. If the market rallies to twenty-seven dollars, the option must at least be worth $2 because you can exercise your right at the agreed amount of twenty-five. So, even though the shares only went up 3.8% you *doubled* your money because you can sell back the option for two dollars ($2). Go to TrendsUniversity.com and look for our DVD series for more details on options pricing.

Limited Risk

One of the biggest advantages option trading has over stock trading is to be able to take a view on market direction with limited risk while at the same time having unlimited profit potential. This is because option buyers have the right, not the obligation, to exercise the contract for the stock at the exercise price. If the stock price at the time of expiration doesn't offer a profitable situation, the buyer will forfeit his or her right and simply let the contract expire worthless. Let me give you an illustration.

Remember our initial example of Jerry buying an Apple Inc (AAPL) call option? The following are details of Jerry's trade using appropriate trade jargon:

- Underlying: AAPL
- Type: Call Option
- Position: Long (i.e., bought the contract)
- Strike Price: $25
- Expiry Date: May 25

At the time of the trade, the underlying AAPL shares were trading around $30. The call option contract has a current market value of $6.50—also known as the *premium*.

From the above information, you can conclude that Jerry will make a profit if AAPL is trading above $31.50 after May 25. Why $31.50? This amount is the break even point. Jerry bought the $25 strike price call option and, in doing so, paid $6.50 for the right to buy the stock at the contracted price of twenty-five dollars. Add the strike price amount to the premium price and the sum is the break even price (e.g., $25 + $6.50 = $31.50). To make a profit, Jerry needs the stock to trade *higher* than the break even price by the contract's expiration date.

A Profitable Trade

If AAPL shares are trading at forty dollars by May 25, then you exercise you right to call the shares from the option seller. Then you will be assigned AAPL shares at the exercise price of twenty-five dollars, which is the same as if you actually bought the shares on the open market for $25.

In the case where you decide to exercise your right and take delivery of the shares, you have to pay the full amount for the shares. To figure your total cost benefit, take the number of purchased option contracts, multiply by the contract size, then multiply by the exercise price. If you are planning to hold onto option contracts until expiry and take delivery, make sure you have the cash!

To make it a profitable trade, let's say that AAPL shares are trading at the stock exchange for $40. You purchased the shares under the option contract at a value of $25 each. You can sell them in the open market or through your broker and take a profit of $8.50 per share! Why $8.50? Remember that premiums must be paid. A quick calculation of the current market value of the stock minus the strike price will give you

174

the value of the call option at expiration (e.g., $40 - $25 = $15). Take the value of option at expiration and subtract the cost of the premium to figure your profit (e.g., $15 - $6.50 = $8.50.)

Think about what happens as the underlying price continues to rise. You continue to make more and more money once the stock price has exceeded the break even point.

What about the downside risk?

A Losing Trade

Let's imagine at expiration AAPL shares are trading *below* our exercise price of twenty-five dollars at, say, $20. Will you decide to exercise your right and take delivery of the shares and pay $25 per share? No. They're only worth $20. Let the option contract expire worthless...gladly.

What have you lost? You lost the premium that you paid to the seller, which in this example was $6.50. That's all. The loss of the initial premium was much less than if the stock had plummeted and you lost your entire investment. Remember there is a multiplier in options trades of 100 so in this example the amount is ($6.50X100=$650) for one contract.

What if the stock market were to crash and AAPL shares were trading at $5 at the time of expiration? You would do the same as if the shares were trading at $20—do nothing. Just let the option contract expire worthless and accept the loss of your premium.

Limited Risk Combined with Unlimited Profit Potential

Using leverage with option contracts not only limits your risk but also leaves you open to make unlimited profit should stocks rally. We say "unlimited profit" because theoretically stocks could go up forever. In reality, unlimited growth won't happen. Still, at any time stock values can climb to staggering levels, and in some cases rise thousands of percentage points.

Not all option strategies have this payoff benefit. Only if you are buying options can you limit your risk. Option sellers experience the opposite result. Writers who are not covered (who don't own the stock) have *unlimited risk* with limited profit potential.

So, why would anybody want to sell options? You can learn more about advanced option strategies in our DVD series at TrendsUniversity.com.

MTS™ Strategies for Options

Buying Options to Sell Options

In almost all cases options traders buy options only to sell them later for a profit. Very rarely will a trader actually *exercise* an option because it is important to maintain the leverage benefit that options provide. In this section, I'll show you prime examples of buying and selling calls and puts. The purpose is to demonstrate how MTS™ system signals bring your attention to opportunities to buy and sell options with increased trading leverage. In each example, you will buy an option and then sell it before expiration.

Buying Calls when MTS™ Gives Bullish/Bull Market Signals

The best market condition for buying call options are Bull markets. The market is Bullish/Bull Market when the majority of stocks are trending and rallying higher. When trading stocks or options, you want to stack as many odds in your favor as possible. This being said, it doesn't mean you can't buy call options in a Bear market or in an extremely oversold market that's looking for a bounce. The probability of success for buying call options in a Bear or oversold market is much smaller.

Locating Candidate Stocks within the MTS™ System

There are several ways to find candidate stocks. You can locate BUY signals for qualified stocks using the MTS™ system's Stock Screener or by using predefined *MuscleStock* scans. Additionally, you can locate an ST Trend UP signal for a stock of your own choosing within the MTS™ system. For more information on the Stock Screener and predefined scans, see *Chapter 3: Identifying High Probability Trades using Market Trend Signal™*.

Your objective is to find trade set ups and find them on demand, right? I can be impatient and know the need to find a trade that could work for me today. The MTS™ system scans for stocks that will meet optimal buying criteria at that moment. Find a stock that has a high reward to risk by looking at a stock's performance over the past year or two using back testing. Another great practice is to look for trades that have high average gains, low average losses, and high trade expectancy. *Spring Loaded* and *New Buys* and are good *MuscleStock* scans you can use to find qualified stocks for trade call options.

Trading Only "In the Money" (ITM) or "At the Money" (ATM) Options

Options that are "in the money" (ITM) have much more intrinsic value which means they will follow the price changes in the stock much more closely than options that are "out of the money." Out of the money options are called "out of the money" (OTM) for a reason: if you trade them very often, you will be *out of money*.

Trading Options with Expirations of Three Months or Less

Most of the *time value* associated with an option contract is lost in the last two months until expiration. There is no need to spend additional money strictly to "buy time." Most MTS™ trades are expected to make trending moves for 2 to eight weeks before a significant correction will occur. This is obviously not going to be the case for all stocks tracked, but on average this will be true. Therefore, buying an option that expires any later than three months from the date of purchase is not maximizing the leverage that the option offers. If the trend looks to continue, you can always sell the options you have and buy new options with a different strike price and expiration month on the same stock.

Setting Up a Buy Stop Limit Order with Your Broker

Most brokers will now allow criteria for options to be set up just the same as you would with stocks. When available, stop orders, limit orders, and contingent orders should be used for your option trades.

Attaching Contingent Stop Loss Orders to the Buy Order

Another best practice is to set up a contingent stop loss order and attach it to the Buy order, whenever possible. Once the Buy signal is triggered, set the stop with a specific option price or loss percentage—any amount between fifty and 100% loss is a good stop loss percentage to begin. Monitor trades once a day in your watch list to determine if a trade adjustment is necessary.

As a general money management rule, you should not allocate more than ten percent of your investment capital to any *one* trade. An even more conservative allocation is 5% of your account. There will be occasions where the stock will not move above the strike price by the time the option contract expires. The option will expire worthless. In this case, any money you have allocated to this trade will be a total loss.

Total losses can be both good and bad. They're bad because you lose all your money. On the other hand, they're good because you always know your exact risk. If you have $10,000 to trade options and use ten percent, i.e. a thousand dollars on one option trade, you already know that the absolute worst case scenario you could face is losing 100% of your investment amount or a $1,000. You cannot lose any more money than a hundred percent of your investment. If you go into the trade with this as your acceptable loss limit on the option trade, it is called a "100% stop," which gives you the flexibility to allow some volatility in the stock while not being overly concerned with your level of risk if the trade moves against you.

In the case of a call option, this means the stock value goes down. You may also prefer to cut the loss at fifty percent. If you had a thousand dollars at risk, you would sell the options once they lost half of their value, i.e. $500. If you paid $10 per contract, you would set up a stop of five dollars with your broker.

Selling Half the Position when the Trade Doubles

When trading options, it's always best to remember the phrase "a bird in the hand is worth two in the bush," which is a phrase meaning that you're better off to have something, rather than take a risk and lose everything.

Options gains can be wiped out quickly, even because of small moves in the stock. The choice to take some portion of your profits *every time* on the trade position is considered a little against the trend following methodology. In trend following stocks, we want to stay in the trade as long as possible while the stock is moving favorably for us. The advantage with stocks and ETFs is there is no expiration date, so we can afford to have time on our side. Options expire, and because of the ever-present decay of time, there may not be enough time to recover losses in a trade where stock prices have moved lower. The bottom line is to take the gains in the option trade along the way.

Selling all Contracts on a Signal Change to HOLD or ST Trend Down

The "bird in the hand" phrase also applies to the situation when the stock trades down enough to trigger a HOLD or ST Trend Down in the MTS™ system. The up trend may be stalling or reversing entirely. Don't wait around to see what happens. Take out any gains or take any remaining capital left in the trade on these signals and look to enter another trade that may be providing a better trade set up.

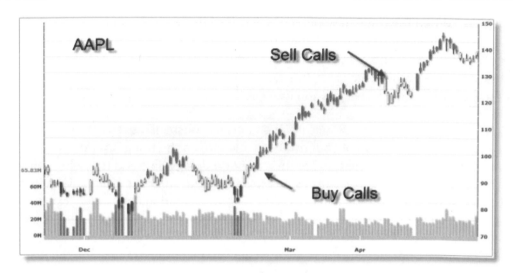

Figure 8.1. An example of when to buy call options when following the MTS™ rules for buying call options.

The MTS™ Process for Buying Call Options

Use these simple steps to ensure a better buying strategy.

1. Buy calls when MTS™ has a Bullish/Bull market condition,
2. Locate the BUY signal on a stock in the MTS™ system using the Stock Screener or *MuscleStock* scans,
3. Or locate the ST Trend UP signal on a stock in the MTS™ system using the Stock Screener or *MuscleStock* scans,
4. Trade only "in the money" (ITM) or "at the money" (ATM) options,
5. Trade options with expirations of 3 months or less,
6. Set up a buy stop limit order with your broker,
7. Set up a contingent stop loss order and attach it to the Buy order (when possible). Once the Buy signal is triggered, set the stop with a specific option price or percent loss (fifty or 100% loss are both good places to start),
8. Monitor trades once a day in your watch list to determine if a trade adjustment is necessary,

9. When the trade has doubled, sell half of the position, and
10. Sell all contracts on a signal change to HOLD or ST Trend Down.

Figure 8.2. An example of where to buy put options using the MTS™ rules for buying put options.

The MTS™ Process for Buying Put Options

Use these simple steps to ensure a better buying strategy. You're looking for the exact opposite conditions with puts as you are with calls.

1. Buy puts when MTS™ has a Bearish/Bear market condition,
2. Locate the SELL signal on a stock in the MTS™ system using the Stock Screener or *MuscleStock* scans,
3. Or locate the ST Trend Down signal on a stock in the MTS™ system using the Stock Screener or *MuscleStock* scans,
4. Trade only "in the money" (ITM) or "at the money" (ATM) options,
5. Trade options with expirations of 3 months or less,
6. Set up a buy stop limit order with your broker,

7. Set up a contingent stop loss order and attach it to the Buy order (when possible). Once the Buy signal is triggered, set the stop with a specific option price or percent loss (fifty or 100% loss are both good places to start),
8. Monitor trades once a day in your watch list to determine if a trade adjustment is necessary,
9. When the trade has doubled sell half of the position, and
10. Sell all contracts on a change to HOLD or ST Trend Up.

Protective Puts

Another reason investors may use options is for portfolio insurance. Option contracts can give investors a method to protect his or her downside probability in the event of a stock market crash. One example of this is called a "protective put."

A protective put strategy has a very similar payoff profile compared to the long call. Your maximum loss is limited to the premium paid for the option while maintaining the advantage of having unlimited profit potential. Protective puts are ideal for investors who are very risk-averse, i.e. investors who hold stock and are concerned about stock corrections.

If the stock sells off rapidly, put option values will *increase* while the value of the stock will decrease. If the combined position is hedged, then the profits of the put options will offset losses.

In the case where the market rises substantially past the exercise price of the put option, the put will expire worthless while the stock position increases. Consider that the loss of the put position is limited, while profits gained from the increase in stock position are unlimited. The losses of put option contracts compared to the gains from high-performing stocks do not offset each other. Profits gained from an increased value of an underlying stock certainly outweigh any loss you may experience because you decide to allow the put option to expire. Your gains will cover the loss of option premiums.

The MTS™ Process for Buying Protective Puts

Use these simple steps to ensure a better buying strategy.

1. Buy puts on a stock that you own and would like to keep. Make sure that the stock has been trending higher and has a BUY rating that has changed to HOLD or SELL,
2. Trade "in the money," (ITM) "at the money," (ATM) or "out of the money" (OTM) options,
3. Trade options with expirations of 3 months or less,
4. Set up a buy stop limit order with your broker,
5. Monitor trades once a day in your watch list to determine if a trade adjustment is necessary,
6. If the stock is still a SELL rating and expiration of the put is in 2 weeks or less, sell the puts and buy more puts with a new expiration date and strike price, and
7. Once the stock moves from a HOLD to a BUY rating, buy more of the stock shares with the gains from the puts.

Selling (Writing) Covered Calls

Selling (writing) covered calls is a strategy where you own the stock and you sell call options against the stock you own. The call is "covered" because you own the stock. You can generate extra income from a stock you own that may not currently be trending. Stocks that have been trending with a BUY rating and move to HOLD are candidates for selling covered calls. The ideal situation for this trade is a stock that is trending higher but is consolidating or correcting with a HOLD rating for a period of weeks.

When you sell a call you are selling to someone else the right to buy the stock for a fixed price (strike price). If the stock moves higher, you will be obligated to sell shares of stock to the call buyer if they decide to exercise their option to buy the stock. This is known as being "called away" or "called out" of the stock.

By selling (writing) covered calls, you're making monthly income by selling upside potential of stock to speculators. When you write covered calls you must do one of the following:

- If exercised, sell the underlying stock to the option buyer at the strike price any time before expiration;
- Buy the calls back on the open market before the option buyer exercises his right; or
- Let the calls expire unexercised (on the third Friday of the expiration month).

There is one way you can lose money through this strategy, and that is if the stock goes down at a fast rate. You can always place a stop order that will sell your stock and buy back your call option if the stock starts to lose money. In most cases, the amount you would lose on the stock would be offset somewhat by the amount you gain on the option.

Writing "In the Money" (ITM) Covered Calls

If you expect some sideways movement in a stock based on a HOLD signal, write covered calls. The advantage of writing "in the money" (ITM) covered calls is better downside protection. You make a profit regardless of the direction of the stock.

For instance, if you purchase one hundred shares of stock for $10.75 per share, you could write a ten dollar ITM covered call and get a premium of, say, $1.50. If the stock closes above ten dollars at option expiration, it will be called for $10. You would still make a profit because your cost is only $9.25. Otherwise, if the stock doesn't close above $10 at option expiration, it wouldn't be called out. At that point, you would either sell the stock or write a covered call against it for next month, which is called "rolling out". As long as the stock's value is above $9.25, you profit.

"In the Money" (ITM) Covered Calls Example			
		Cost	Return
Buy stock (market)	$10.75 x 1,000	$10,750.00	--
Sell $10.00 covered calls	$1.50 x 1,000	--	$1,500.00
Sell stock (called)	$10.00 x 1,000	--	$10,000.00
Approximate Commissions		$56.00	--
		$10,806.00	$11,500.00

Table 8.2. "In the money" covered call transaction returns $694, yielding 6.5% in 36 days or less with $750 downside protection.

Writing "At the Money" (ATM) or "Out of the Money" (OTM) Covered Calls

If market conditions are Bullish and the stock you're following in the MTS™ system back testing has shown historically large average gains, write "out of the money" (OTM) covered calls while you own the stock.

If you purchase one hundred shares of stock for $4.75 per share, you could write a five dollar OTM covered call and get a premium of, say, $0.50. If the stock closes above $5 at option expiration, it would be called for five dollars, producing a $0.25 capital gain in addition to the premium. Otherwise, if the stock does not close above $5 at option expiration, it won't be called. At that point, you would either sell the stock or write covered calls against it for next month. As long as the stock's value is above $4.25, you profit.

"Out of the Money" (OTM) Covered Calls Example

		Cost	Return
Buy stock (market)	$4.75 x 200	$950.00	--
Sell $5.00 covered calls	$0.50 x 200	--	$100.00
Sell stock (called)	$5.00 x 200	--	$1,000.00
Approximate Commissions		$28.00	--
		$978.00	$1,100.00

Table 8.3. "Out of the money" covered call transaction returns $122, yielding 12.5% in 36 days or less.

Trade Adjustments

If the call is close to expiration you probably have a good idea whether or not you are going to get called out of that option. If the option is "in the money" (ITM) or the strike price is below the price of the stock then you will probably be called out, unless of course you buy back the option.

But what if the option is "out of the money" (OTM) and is nearly worthless? There are many times when the call on a stock would be worth $.05 and still has a week before expiration. In this case, you can choose to either let the option sit and slowly make that extra $.05 or roll your options to a later date.

If you choose to roll your option, you will buy back your option and sell another option with a later expiration date. For example, if the next month's option contract is selling at eighty cents and your current call option is trading at $.05, it could definitely be worth it to buy it back for a nickel and sell another one for $.80.

This could potentially be more profitable than letting the other option melt away before buying the next month's option. The process of buying back your option and selling (writing) another option with a different expiration date or strike price is referred to as "rolling out."

The MTS™ Process for Selling Covered Call Options

Use these simple steps to ensure a better buying strategy.

1. Sell (write) calls when MTS™ has a Bullish/Bull market condition
2. Locate a HOLD signal on a stock in the MTS™ system using the Stock Screener or *MuscleStock* scans or watch for the HOLD signal on a stock you own,
3. Trade options with expirations of 2 months or less,
4. Set up a sell stop limit order with your broker,
5. Monitor trades once a day in your watch list to determine if a trade adjustment is necessary,
6. Be prepared to buy back the call or sell the stock if called out,
7. If the stock has declined and you don't want to keep it, close your call by buying it back and sell the stock, or roll out or roll down, and
8. Roll out the trade by buying back the option and selling more contracts with a new expiration month and/or strike price.

Notes and Comments

Notes and Comments

Notes and Comments

References

William J. O'Neil, *"How to Make Money in Stocks: A Winning System in Good Times and Bad, Fourth Edition,"* McGraw-Hill; Fourth Edition (May 18, 2009).

Referenced Investment Firms/Companies on the US:NYSE (alphabetical):

Advanced Micro Devices Inc (AMD)
Aeropostale Inc (ARO)
AK Steel Holding Corp (AKS)
Almost Family Inc (AFAM)
Apple Inc (AAPL)
AT&T Communications Inc (ATT)
Avis Budget Group Inc (CAR)
Bear Stearns (BSC) [former]
Beazer Homes USA Inc (BZH)
BJs Restaurants Inc (BJRI)
Boeing Co (BA)
Boise, Inc (BZ)
Bon-Ton Stores Inc (BONT)
Cal Maine Foods Inc (CALM)
CalAmp Corp (CAMP)
Costco Wholesale (COST)
Dollar Thrifty Automotive Group Inc (DTG)
Entercom Communications Corp (ETM)
Ezcorp Inc (EZPW)
Fannie Mae (FNM)
Ford Motor Company (F)
Freeport McMoRan Copper & Gold Inc (FCX)
General Electric Company (GE)
General Motors Corp (GM)
Goldman Sachs Group Inc (GS)
Google Inc (GOOG)
Hansen Natural Corp (HANS)
Human Genome Sciences Inc (HGSI)

continued

Intel Corporation (INTC)
International Business Machines Corp (IBM)
iShares COMEX Gold Trust (IAU)
iShares Dow Jones US Financial Sector (IYF)
Lehman Brothers Holdings Inc (LEH) [former]
Medifast Inc (MED)
Microsoft Corp (MSFT)
Northeast Utilities (NU)
Office Depot Inc (ODP)
RINO International Corp (RINO)
Smart Modular Technologies Inc. (SMOD)
Sunrise Senior Living Inc (SRZ)
TASER International Inc (TASR)
Tenneco Inc (TEN)
TRW Automotive Holdings Corp (TRW)
Valassis Communications Inc (VCI)
Walt Disney Company (DIS)
Washington Mutual Inc (WM)

* Please refer to copyright information and investment advisory statement regarding liability and risk. All publicly held companies referenced herein are sole entities having no stake in the MTS™system or related learning materials.

Appendix

10 year performance

Back Test	Equity Curve	StockSymbol	afam

Trade Stats for **AFAM** Current Signal Buy Please select buy/sell criteria

Number of Trades	43	Trade expectancy	$961.68
Total Profit amount	$250,157.34	Trade expectancy%	9.61%
Total Loss amount	$113,254.69	Annual Trade expectancy	$4,040.42
Total Profit or Total Loss	$136,902.65	Annual Trade expectancy%	40.40%
Avg Profit on Winners	$14,715.14	Largest profit	$60,227.44
Avg Loss on Losers	$4,355.95	Largest loss	$18,242.14
Total Net % gain or loss	1369.03%	Avg days in trade	48
Aver % gain on Winners	35.89%	Avg days between trades	38
Aver % loss on Losers	7.56%		
Reward to Risk Ratio	4.75		
Number of Trades Per year	4.2		
Number of Winners	17		
Number of Losers	26		
Winning Percentage	39.53		

☑ Long
Buy   Sell
Buy ▼   Sell ▼

☐ Short
Sell   Buy
Sell ▼   Buy ▼

Investment dollars: 10000
Additions on Signals
☑ Compound original invesment
☐ Use fixed amount on new signal

Start date 01/01/2000   End date 03/24/2010   Query

Appendix Figure 1. Almost Family Inc (AFAM) trade statistics from 01/01/2000 through 03/24/2010.

Back Test	Equity Curve	StockSymbol	aks

Trade Stats for **AKS** Current Signal Buy Please select buy/sell criteria

Number of Trades	34	Trade expectancy	$1474.47
Total Profit amount	$222,756.05	Trade expectancy%	14.74%
Total Loss amount	$50,326.56	Annual Trade expectancy	$4,900.17
Total Profit or Total Loss	$172,429.50	Annual Trade expectancy%	49.00%
Avg Profit on Winners	$12,375.34	Largest profit	$77,331.78
Avg Loss on Losers	$3,145.41	Largest loss	$21,906.37
Total Net % gain or loss	1724.29%	Avg days in trade	64
Aver % gain on Winners	38.25%	Avg days between trades	47
Aver % loss on Losers	11.70%		
Reward to Risk Ratio	3.27		
Number of Trades Per year	3.3		
Number of Winners	18		
Number of Losers	16		
Winning Percentage	52.94		

☑ Long
Buy   Sell
Buy ▼   Sell ▼

☐ Short
Sell   Buy
Sell ▼   Buy ▼

Investment dollars: 10000
Additions on Signals
☑ Compound original invesment
☐ Use fixed amount on new signal

Start date 01/01/2000   End date 03/24/2010   Query

Appendix Figure 2. AK Steel Holding Corp (AKS) trade statistics from 01/01/2000 through 03/24/2010.

Back Test	Equity Curve	StockSymbol	amd		Please select buy/sell criteria

Trade Stats for **AMD**   Current Signal   Buy

Number of Trades	38	Trade expectancy	$1169.48
Total Profit amount	$197,469.72	Trade expectancy%	11.69%
Total Loss amount	$87,749.70	Annual Trade expectancy	$4,343.43
Total Profit or Total Loss	$109,720.02	Annual Trade expectancy%	43.43%
Avg Profit on Winners	$13,164.65	Largest profit	$28,623.32
Avg Loss on Losers	$3,815.20	Largest loss	$10,604.59
Total Net % gain or loss	1097.20%	Avg days in trade	47
Aver % gain on Winners	46.07%	Avg days between trades	53
Aver % loss on Losers	10.73%		
Reward to Risk Ratio	4.30		
Number of Trades Per year	3.7		
Number of Winners	15		
Number of Losers	23		
Winning Percentage	39.47		

☑ Long
Buy — Sell
□ Short
Sell — Buy
Investment dollars: 10000
Additions on Signals:
☑ Compound original invesment
□ Use fixed amount on new signal

Start date 01/01/2000   End date 03/24/2010   Query

Appendix Figure 3. Advanced Micro Devices Inc (AMD) trade statistics from 01/01/2000 through 03/24/2010.

Back Test	Equity Curve	StockSymbol	ba		Please select buy/sell criteria

Trade Stats for **BA**   Current Signal   Buy

Number of Trades	34	Trade expectancy	$521.61
Total Profit amount	$49,908.33	Trade expectancy%	5.21%
Total Loss amount	$16,072.43	Annual Trade expectancy	$1,732.01
Total Profit or Total Loss	$33,835.90	Annual Trade expectancy%	17.32%
Avg Profit on Winners	$2,626.75	Largest profit	$12,064.54
Avg Loss on Losers	$1,071.50	Largest loss	$3,156.15
Total Net % gain or loss	338.36%	Avg days in trade	63
Aver % gain on Winners	13.48%	Avg days between trades	45
Aver % loss on Losers	5.25%		
Reward to Risk Ratio	2.57		
Number of Trades Per year	3.3		
Number of Winners	19		
Number of Losers	15		
Winning Percentage	55.88		

☑ Long
Buy — Sell
□ Short
Sell — Buy
Investment dollars: 10000
Additions on Signals:
☑ Compound original invesment
□ Use fixed amount on new signal

Start date 01/01/2000   End date 03/24/2010   Query

Appendix Figure 4. Boeing Co (BA) trade statistics from 01/01/2000 through 03/24/2010.

| Back Test | Equity Curve | StockSymbol | bjri |

Trade Stats for   BJRI   Current Signal   Buy   Please select buy/sell criteria

Number of Trades	45	Trade expectancy	$604.97	☑ Long
Total Profit amount	$126,458.53	Trade expectancy%	6.04%	
Total Loss amount	$76,637.04	Annual Trade expectancy	$2,657.57	Buy Sell
Total Profit or Total Loss	$49,821.49	Annual Trade expectancy%	26.58%	Buy ▼ Sell ▼
Avg Profit on Winners	$6,021.83	Largest profit	$20,534.67	
Avg Loss on Losers	$3,193.21	Largest loss	$10,687.76	☐ Short
Total Net % gain or loss	498.21%	Avg days in trade	45	Sell Buy
Aver % gain on Winners	21.27%	Avg days between trades	35	Sell ▼ Buy ▼
Aver % loss on Losers	7.27%			
Reward to Risk Ratio	2.93			Investment dollars: 10000
Number of Trades Per year	4.4			
Number of Winners	21			Additions on Signals
Number of Losers	24			☑ Compound original invesment
Winning Percentage	46.67			☐ Use fixed amount on new signal

Start date 01/01/2000   End date 03/24/2010   Query

Appendix Figure 5. BJs Restaurants Inc (BJRI) trade statistics from 01/01/2000 through 03/24/2010.

| Back Test | Equity Curve | StockSymbol | bzh |

Trade Stats for   BZH   Current Signal   Buy   Please select buy/sell criteria

Number of Trades	34	Trade expectancy	$1158.19	☑ Long
Total Profit amount	$264,260.56	Trade expectancy%	11.58%	
Total Loss amount	$125,543.05	Annual Trade expectancy	$3,849.66	Buy Sell
Total Profit or Total Loss	$138,717.51	Annual Trade expectancy%	38.50%	Buy ▼ Sell ▼
Avg Profit on Winners	$13,908.45	Largest profit	$105,311.45	
Avg Loss on Losers	$8,369.54	Largest loss	$39,839.22	☐ Short
Total Net % gain or loss	1387.18%	Avg days in trade	58	Sell Buy
Aver % gain on Winners	29.02%	Avg days between trades	54	Sell ▼ Buy ▼
Aver % loss on Losers	10.51%			
Reward to Risk Ratio	2.76			Investment dollars: 10000
Number of Trades Per year	3.3			
Number of Winners	19			Additions on Signals
Number of Losers	15			☑ Compound original invesment
Winning Percentage	55.88			☐ Use fixed amount on new signal

Start date 01/01/2000   End date 03/24/2010   Query

Appendix Figure 6. Beazer Homes USA Inc (BZH) trade statistics from 01/01/2000 through 03/24/2010.

	Back Test	Equity Curve	StockSymbol	calm		

Trade Stats for	**CALM**		Current Signal	Buy		Please select buy/sell criteria
Number of Trades	38	Trade expectancy	$2331.21		☑ **Long**	
Total Profit amount	$157,421.27	Trade expectancy%	23.31%		Buy	Sell
Total Loss amount	$63,964.51	Annual Trade expectancy	$8,660.85		Buy ▾	Sell ▾
Total Profit or Total Loss	$93,456.77	Annual Trade expectancy%	86.61%			
Avg Profit on Winners	$9,260.07	Largest profit	$52,686.54			
Avg Loss on Losers	$3,045.93	Largest loss	$14,844.06		☐ **Short**	
Total Net % gain or loss	934.57%	Avg days in trade	54		Sell	Buy
Aver % gain on Winners	62.09%	Avg days between trades	46		Sell ▾	Buy ▾
Aver % loss on Losers	8.08%					
Reward to Risk Ratio	7.69				Investment dollars:	10000
Number of Trades Per year	3.7					
Number of Winners	17				Additions on Signals	
Number of Losers	21					
Winning Percentage	44.74				☑ Compound original invesment	
					☐ Use fixed amount on new signal	

Start date 01/01/2000   End date 03/24/2010   Query

Appendix Figure 7. Cal Maine Foods Inc (CALM) trade statistics from 01/01/2000 through 03/24/2010.

	Back Test	Equity Curve	StockSymbol	DTG		

Trade Stats for	**DTG**		Current Signal	Buy		Please select buy/sell criteria
Number of Trades	38	Trade expectancy	$5018.61		☑ **Long**	
Total Profit amount	$244,902.15	Trade expectancy%	50.18%		Buy	Sell
Total Loss amount	$44,264.81	Annual Trade expectancy	$18,654.43		Buy ▾	Sell ▾
Total Profit or Total Loss	$200,637.33	Annual Trade expectancy%	186.54%			
Avg Profit on Winners	$14,406.01	Largest profit	$151,866.97			
Avg Loss on Losers	$2,107.85	Largest loss	$8,724.12		☐ **Short**	
Total Net % gain or loss	2006.37%	Avg days in trade	57		Sell	Buy
Aver % gain on Winners	124.26%	Avg days between trades	40		Sell ▾	Buy ▾
Aver % loss on Losers	9.78%					
Reward to Risk Ratio	12.71				Investment dollars:	10000
Number of Trades Per year	3.7					
Number of Winners	17				Additions on Signals	
Number of Losers	21					
Winning Percentage	44.74				☑ Compound original invesment	
					☐ Use fixed amount on new signal	

Start date 01/03/2000   End date 03/24/2010   Query

Appendix Figure 8. Dollar Thrifty Automotive Group Inc (DTG) trade statistics from 01/03/2000 through 03/24/2010.

Back Test	Equity Curve	StockSymbol	ezpw

| Trade Stats for | **EZPW** | Current Signal | Buy |

				Please select buy/sell criteria
Number of Trades	35	Trade expectancy	$1393.53	☑ Long
Total Profit amount	$351,153.73	Trade expectancy%	13.93%	Buy — Sell
Total Loss amount	$214,884.23	Annual Trade expectancy	$4,767.10	Buy ▾ — Sell ▾
Total Profit or Total Loss	$136,269.50	Annual Trade expectancy%	47.67%	
Avg Profit on Winners	$27,011.83	Largest profit	$101,081.58	
Avg Loss on Losers	$9,767.46	Largest loss	$29,851.78	☐ Short
Total Net % gain or loss	1362.70%	Avg days in trade	57	Sell — Buy
Aver % gain on Winners	53.89%	Avg days between trades	48	Sell ▾ — Buy ▾
Aver % loss on Losers	9.67%			
Reward to Risk Ratio	5.57			Investment dollars: 10000
Number of Trades Per year	3.4			
Number of Winners	13			Additions on Signals
Number of Losers	22			☑ Compound original invesment
Winning Percentage	37.14			☐ Use fixed amount on new signal

| Start date | 01/01/2000 | End date | 03/24/2010 | | Query |

Appendix Figure 9. Ezcorp Inc (EZPW) trade statistics from 01/01/2000 through 03/24/2010.

Back Test	Equity Curve	StockSymbol	fcx

| Trade Stats for | **FCX** | Current Signal | Buy |

				Please select buy/sell criteria
Number of Trades	30	Trade expectancy	$1263.68	☑ Long
Total Profit amount	$204,758.07	Trade expectancy%	12.63%	Buy — Sell
Total Loss amount	$69,918.89	Annual Trade expectancy	$3,704.75	Buy ▾ — Sell ▾
Total Profit or Total Loss	$134,839.18	Annual Trade expectancy%	37.05%	
Avg Profit on Winners	$13,650.54	Largest profit	$42,667.64	
Avg Loss on Losers	$4,661.26	Largest loss	$21,557.64	☐ Short
Total Net % gain or loss	1348.39%	Avg days in trade	77	Sell — Buy
Aver % gain on Winners	32.44%	Avg days between trades	42	Sell ▾ — Buy ▾
Aver % loss on Losers	7.16%			
Reward to Risk Ratio	4.53			Investment dollars: 10000
Number of Trades Per year	2.9			
Number of Winners	15			Additions on Signals
Number of Losers	15			☑ Compound original invesment
Winning Percentage	50.00			☐ Use fixed amount on new signal

| Start date | 01/01/2000 | End date | 03/24/2010 | | Query |

Appendix Figure 10. Freeport McMoRan Copper and Gold Inc (FCX) trade statistics from 01/01/2000 through 03/24/2010.

Market Trend Signal™
Market Timing - Trend Following - Stock Ratings

Appendix

| Back Test | Equity Curve | StockSymbol | hgsi |

Trade Stats for HGSI   Current Signal Buy   Please select buy/sell criteria

Number of Trades	38	Trade expectancy	$1486.90
Total Profit amount	$121,380.64	Trade expectancy%	14.86%
Total Loss amount	$28,290.36	Annual Trade expectancy	$5,524.21
Total Profit or Total Loss	$93,090.28	Annual Trade expectancy%	55.24%
Avg Profit on Winners	$6,388.45	Largest profit	$55,252.41
Avg Loss on Losers	$1,488.97	Largest loss	$4,342.83
Total Net % gain or loss	930.90%	Avg days in trade	47
Aver % gain on Winners	40.28%	Avg days between trades	51
Aver % loss on Losers	10.55%	Longest nbr of consecutive winners	
Reward to Risk Ratio	3.82	Longest nbr of consecutive losers	
Number of Trades Per year	3.7	Largest Drawdown	
Number of Winners	19	Avg Drawdown	
Number of Losers	19		
Winning Percentage	50.00		

☑ Long
  Buy   Sell
  [Buy ▾]   [Sell ▾]

☐ Short
  Sell   Buy
  [Sell ▾] [Buy ▾]

Investment dollars: 10000
Additions on Signals
☑ Compound original invesment
☐ Use fixed amount on new signal

Start date 01/03/2000   End date 03/24/2010

Query

Appendix Figure 11. Human Genome Sciences Inc (HGSI) trade statistics from 01/03/2000 through 03/24/2010.

| Back Test | Equity Curve | StockSymbol | ODP |

Trade Stats for ODP   Current Signal Buy   Please select buy/sell criteria

Number of Trades	32	Trade expectancy	$895.20
Total Profit amount	$91,852.81	Trade expectancy%	8.95%
Total Loss amount	$31,924.39	Annual Trade expectancy	$2,800.32
Total Profit or Total Loss	$59,928.42	Annual Trade expectancy%	28.00%
Avg Profit on Winners	$6,123.52	Largest profit	$28,831.68
Avg Loss on Losers	$1,877.91	Largest loss	$7,607.08
Total Net % gain or loss	599.28%	Avg days in trade	65
Aver % gain on Winners	28.11%	Avg days between trades	54
Aver % loss on Losers	7.95%		
Reward to Risk Ratio	3.54		
Number of Trades Per year	3.1		
Number of Winners	15		
Number of Losers	17		
Winning Percentage	46.88		

☑ Long
  Buy   Sell
  [Buy ▾]   [Sell ▾]

☐ Short
  Sell   Buy
  [Sell ▾] [Buy ▾]

Investment dollars: 10000
Additions on Signals
☑ Compound original invesment
☐ Use fixed amount on new signal

Start date 01/01/2000   End date 03/24/2010

Query

Appendix Figure 12. Office Depot Inc (ODP) trade statistics from 01/01/2000 through 03/24/2010.

| Back Test | Equity Curve | StockSymbol | SRZ |

| Trade Stats for | **SRZ** | | | Current Signal | Buy | | | | Please select buy/sell criteria |

Number of Trades	36	Trade expectancy	$746.66	☑ Long			
Total Profit amount	$75,250.82	Trade expectancy%	7.46%	Buy		Sell	
Total Loss amount	$31,272.72	Annual Trade expectancy	$2,627.30				
Total Profit or Total Loss	$43,978.11	Annual Trade expectancy%	26.27%	Buy ▾		Sell ▾	
Avg Profit on Winners	$3,960.57	Largest profit	$20,120.87				
Avg Loss on Losers	$1,839.57	Largest loss	$6,405.42	☐ Short			
Total Net % gain or loss	439.78%	Avg days in trade	61	Sell		Buy	
Aver % gain on Winners	21.98%	Avg days between trades	43				
Aver % loss on Losers	8.75%	Longest nbr of consecutive winners		Sell ▾		Buy ▾	
Reward to Risk Ratio	2.51	Longest nbr of consecutive losers					
Number of Trades Per year	3.5	Largest Drawdown		Investment dollars:	10000		
Number of Winners	19	Avg Drawdown					
Number of Losers	17			Additions on Signals			
Winning Percentage	52.78			☑ Compound original invesment			
				☐ Use fixed amount on new signal			

| Start date | 01/03/2000 | End date | 03/24/2010 | | Query |

Appendix Figure 13. Sunrise Senior Living Inc (SRZ) trade statistics from 01/03/2000 through 03/24/2010.

Disclaimer

There is no guarantee past performance will be indicative or future results. No assurance can be given that any implied recommendation will be profitable or will not be subject to losses. All Clients should understand that the results of a particular period will not necessarily be indicative of results in future periods. The results and examples shown in this book and those listed at the www.markettrendsignal.com Web site are based on hypothetical trades. Plainly speaking, these trades were not actually executed. Hypothetical or simulated performance results have certain inherent limitations. Unlike an actual performance record, simulated trades do not represent actual trading. Also, since the trades have not actually been executed, results may have overcompensated or undercompensated for the impact, if any, of certain market factors such as lack of liquidity. Clients may have done better or worse than the results portrayed. No representation is being made that any account will or is likely to achieve profits or losses similar to those shown. No independent party has audited the hypothetical performance contained at this Web site, nor has any independent party undertaken to confirm that they reflect the trading method under the assumptions or conditions specified hereafter. While the results presented at this Web site are based upon certain assumptions believed to reflect actual trading conditions, these assumptions may not include all variables that will affect, or have in the past affected the execution of trades indicated by Market Trend Signal™. Results do not account for commissions or slippage. Because Clients may be involved in trades at different times and may use various exit approaches, they may or may not have received the best available price on the purchase or the sale of a position. The simulation assumes purchase and sale prices believed to be attainable. In actual trading, prices received may or may not be the same as the assumed order prices.

Take your success to the next level

Visit MarketTrendSignal.com to learn more about additional products and services.

Private Mentoring

To enroll in Trends University Private Mentoring Sessions contact us at
1-866-620-2664